The Keymaster and the Music Box

Armando Pazos

Copyright © 2024 by Armando Pazos

All rights reserved.

No part of this book may be reproduced, distributed, or transmitted in any form or by any means, including photocopying, recording, or other electronic or mechanical methods, without the prior written permission of the author, except in the case of brief quotations embodied in critical reviews and specific other noncommercial uses permitted by copyright law.

Contents

Introduction 1
Chapter One: The Arrival 2
Chapter Two: Luscious and Thaddeus 14
Chapter Three: The Sixteenth Birthday 24
Chapter Four: The Secret Place 31
Chapter Five: The Enchanted Couple 39
Chapter Six: The Last Journey 48
Chapter Seven: Zoltar's Return 61
Chapter Eight: The Music Box 73
Chapter Nine: The Secret Mission 86
Chapter Ten: The New Prophecy 93
Chapter Eleven: The Christmas Gift 107
Chapter Twelve: Aura Gate 122
Chapter Thirteen: The Dwarf's Village 129
Chapter Fourteen: The First Task 140
Chapter Fifteen: A Wise Choice 152
Chapter Sixteen: Aurus Wind 164
Chapter Seventeen: The Wrath of Zoltar 173
Chapter Eighteen: The Eye of the Seeker 181
Chapter Nineteen:" The Second Task 191
Chapter Twenty: The Stone's Guardian 200
Chapter Twenty-one: The Scepter of Julius 212
Chapter Twenty-two: Closing the Labyrinths 219
Chapter Twenty-three: The Golden Crossbow 229
Chapter Twenty-four: The Battle for Ethernia 246
Chapter Twenty-five: The New Beginning 265

Introduction

Dear friends, the story you are about to read will remind you once more how, creative, powerful, and unlimited the human imagination is. How many times have you dreamed of or imagined flying over Manhattan on a magic carpet, going back in time to King Arthur's court, or going hundreds of years into the future to drive flying cars and travel to other planets in starships, or even being in a magical place where you are fighting dragons and trolls and swimming with a group of mermaids.

Dreaming is a part of our lives and gives us a reason to believe in what we can do. Therefore, my fellow readers, no matter what happens in your lives, keep dreaming because someday, they may come true....

Chapter One: The Arrival

In the upper-class community of Green Meadows, in the town of Concord, Massachusetts, a few miles outside downtown Boston, stands a beautiful Victorian house, built at the end of the 1920s, with its façade covered in decorative bricks and a tall dome in the middle that makes it look like a small chateau. Pine trees surround its grounds, and the landscaping is always professionally manicured, including a beautiful rose garden, which is the pride of the Logan family. At the front of the house is a stately gated entrance, with a driveway that circles a water fountain right in the middle. This beautiful landmark belongs to the Logan family, a fourth-generation Scottish immigrants who settled in the area in the late 1890s.

Since they came to America, the Logans had been chosen without knowing as the keepers of a secret. This secret lies somewhere in the attic of this beautiful Victorian house, waiting for the arrival of the right Logan, the one marked by the clover, whose destiny will be to uncover this secret and become the Keymaster of a gate that connects our world with a magical place that for many only exists in their imagination.

******

Our story begins about sixteen years ago, on one of the dreariest Thanksgiving Days the Boston area had ever seen. The Logans were preparing to celebrate the traditional holiday, along with some family members, later that day. In the kitchen, Helen, the wife, who was a little over eight months pregnant, was helping her old housekeeper, Mrs. Helga Muller, finish basting the 26-pound turkey they had almost ready in the oven. Suddenly, Lucy, their nearly four-year-old daughter, came into the kitchen scampering with Chester, her golden retriever puppy. Helen told her to stop running, but the little girl was so focused on catching the puppy that she didn't hear her mother's warning. A second later, Lucy tripped over one of the legs of the kitchen table and fell. Helen crouched abruptly to help her daughter when she felt her water break. The little girl screamed in fright, and as she was about to start crying, she looked at her mother and, pointing at the floor, she said, "Mommy, Mommy, you just peed on yourself."

Helen looked at the wet floor and yelled, "Oh my God, my water just broke."

Meanwhile, in the family room, Conrad W. Logan II, the husband, a professor of history at Harvard University and member of a long line of antiques collectors, was sitting on his favorite couch, enjoying a cold beer and watching the football game, the New England Patriots, his favorite team, against the Dallas Cowboys. He had two passions, football being the second. Just when the Patriots were about to score a touchdown, he heard the noise in the kitchen and his daughter screaming; he jumped off the couch and dashed into the kitchen to see what had happened, almost colliding with Mrs. Muller as she was coming out, yelling,

"Mr. Conrad, Mr. Con- Conrad!"

"What's going on, Helga?" He grabbed her before she could fall.

The loyal housekeeper/Nanny, an immigrant from Germany in her early fifties who has been working with Helen's family as her nanny since she was in her twenties, usually stutters when nervous, said, "Hu, hurry up, si sir; you...r-r-r wife water just b-broke."

Conrad Logan, a usually calm man who likes to be prepared in advance for any contingency, had already packed Helen's suitcase and placed it beside the front door. He had also worked out at least two different routes depending on traffic to reach the hospital. But at the moment of truth, he reacted in such a panic that he forgot everything and grabbed his jacket, his car keys, and the suitcase, leaving so quickly that he forgot the essential thing: Helen.

"Oh my God, he did it again!" Helen exclaimed as she walked out of the house, seeing Conrad driving away without her and remembering what happened when Lucy was born. She took a deep breath and went back inside, saying to Mrs. Muller,

"Helga, you won't believe what just happened!"

"Don't tell me, Miss Helen, he le-left again… without you?" the loyal housekeeper answered.

Helen lifted her eyebrows and, chuckling, said,

"Don't worry about me... my dear; he'll notice soon and will return for me!"

Then, Lucy approached her mother and asked, "Where's Daddy?"

Mother and Nanny exchanged a knowing glance and started laughing.

"Let's see how long he takes before noticing that he is alone in the car!" Helen said in a sarcastic tone.

After driving for a couple of minutes, Conrad finally realized he was alone in the car and said, "Oh crap, I did it again."

He immediately turned back, but the rain started falling harder, and it took endless minutes to get home. In the meantime, Helen was waiting in the hall by the front door, pretending to be calm; Lucy and Mrs. Muller were there supporting her. When Conrad finally got home, the three women looked at him like a firing squad ready to shoot. He lifted his arms like begging for forgiveness and, with a nervous smile, said,

"I'm sorry, my dear. I don't know what to say."

"Don't say anything, Conrad. Let's go now," Helen exclaimed.

The rain was coming hard, and it wasn't easy to see the road, forcing Conrad to go very slowly. Helen started having labor pains, making Conrad even more nervous that he completely forgot the route and made a wrong turn a couple of times. They stopped at a red light, which seemed endless. Helen was having another contraction, and when Conrad was about to have a nervous breakdown, the light changed to green. Suddenly, and in the snap of two fingers, the rain calmed down, and like magic, all the traffic lights were turning green as they approached them. Conrad couldn't believe his lucky stars and said,

"I don't know what's going on. I never saw all these lights on green simultaneously; we'll get there soon, dear…"

Meanwhile, Helen's doctor, Dr. Fitzpatrick, was waiting with his team ready; Helen had called him just before leaving her house. As soon as they arrived, Helen was taken directly to one of the delivery rooms, and Conrad, who was still hyper, was taken by the doctor to the closest waiting room, where the doctor told him,

"Easy, my friend… you need to calm down, sit down, and try to relax; I'll check on Helen first and call you when she's ready."

But the doctor didn't come back for almost the next three hours. The baby didn't turn and was in the breech position. Helen wanted to have a natural birth, but the doctor insisted on performing a C-section to protect her and the baby. In the end, Helen prevailed, and she delivered the baby naturally. Both the mother and child were perfectly well. In the waiting room, Conrad was about to have a breakdown because he did not know what was happening with Helen and the baby, so when the doctor came out and gave him the good news, he felt a huge relief. The baby was only 6 ½ pounds and 19 1/2 inches, but he looked healthy and beautiful…too beautiful for a newborn! Then, Conrad was taken immediately to the delivery room.

The Logans could not be happier. Helen cried as she embraced the baby, and Conrad kissed them both. Then, the nurses took the baby and started cleaning him, but when they found a distinctive mark on his left forearm, they called the doctor's attention,

"Doctor, I've never seen anything like this before; it's a perfect clover," one of the nurses said.

"Me neither," said a second one, impressed.

Doctor Fitzpatrick looked at the mark, a perfect four-leaf clover; he paused for a second, then said, "This is truly amazing… I've never seen a birthmark like this before." Then, like a good Irishman, the doctor added, "This boy will be very fortunate… first he was born in a breech position, and now this mark." Without delay, he went on to congratulate Conrad.

"My good friend, you don't only have a beautiful boy, but a special one. Let me show you something!" He brought the baby to him and showed him the birthmark. Conrad was speechless and asked the doctor if everything was okay.

"Don't worry, everything is fine… Do you have a name for him?"

"Yes, Andrew, Andrew Logan, like my late father."

"Nice choice," the doctor replied

At that moment, Conrad remembered the box of cigars he had bought for this occasion. Since the nurses were still attending to Helen, he quickly went to his car to retrieve it. When he returned, he started hugging and giving cigars to everyone he encountered, even people he didn't know. When he got to Helen's room, she was already there, so he kissed her again and said, "Thank you, my dear. You did great. We have a beautiful son."

"You're welcome, sweetheart," Helen answered, looking tired.

By then, the rain had stopped, and the night was quiet. The sky was so clear that the full harvest moon was radiant, and the stars were brighter than ever. Just a few hours earlier, the weather had been dreadful—it was hard to believe.

*****

A few miles away, at the Logans' house, at the exact time when the baby was coming into the world, Mrs. Muller and Lucy were watching TV in the kitchen and having some dessert when suddenly, a series of unusual events started happening. First, a female voice was heard, like a cry of lament. The nanny and Lucy looked at each other without saying a word, but then the cry was heard again, a bit louder. Mrs. Muller grabbed Lucy, ran to the living room, and turned on all the lights, but for the next few minutes, all they could hear was a deep silence, so deep that they listened to each other breathing.

The nanny glanced around, but she couldn't find anything unusual, and seconds later, she heard someone knocking firmly and insistently on the door. Chester, the puppy, began acting agitated, barking and running around the house out of control; Mrs. Muller put Lucy down on the sofa and stuttered, "W-Wait here, Lucy." She went on to see who was at the door; to her surprise, she found a short man with long whiskers dressed in a black suit, a green hat, and a matching tie. The old nanny looked at the man, a little perplexed, and before she could say anything, the man handed her a small leather bag. In a low but fascinating voice, he said, "This is for the Keymaster, give it to him on his sixteenth birthday."

Captivated by that voice, Mrs. Muller took the bag. At that moment, lightning struck near the house, and a strong wind blew, pushing the housekeeper back inside. It was so strong that the woman fell, dropping the leather bag and several ornaments. One of the mirrors by the entrance hall fell to the floor, too, breaking into pieces.

Mrs. Muller stood up and went to close the door, but the mysterious man had disappeared. Utterly Flabbergasted, she stammered, "Wa-what?!" as she looked around without finding a trace of that man.

The Housekeeper closed the door in such a fright that without losing a moment, she grabbed Lucy and went straight to the little girl's bedroom and locked the door from the inside, leaving the ornaments and the pieces of the broken mirror on the floor, but most importantly, the leather bag. The nanny didn't notice that the grandfather clock in the living room stopped at 8 pm when Andy was born. This clock had been in the family for over two hundred years and is usually very reliable. A little later, still agitated, Chester finally calmed down, stopped running in front of the attic's door, and stayed there waiting for someone to come out.

About one hour later, when Mrs. Muller and Lucy were sleeping, the mysterious short man returned, appearing right by the puppy's side. When Chester was about to bark, the man quickly pulled a small flute from his right pocket and started playing a tune that only the dog could hear. Enchanted by the magic tune, the puppy calmed down and immediately followed the man downstairs, where he ordered the puppy to grab the leather bag from the floor and then follow him to the backyard, where the puppy buried it somewhere in the rose garden. Then, with another flute tone, the man ordered the dog to return to the house, and he disappeared again.

******

Later that night. When Conrad came home, he found the broken pieces of the mirror and the ornaments on the floor. He wondered what had happened, but since he didn't want to wake Mrs. Muller, he went to the kitchen to pick up the broom and the dustpan to clean it himself. On the way to the kitchen, he saw the grandfather clock stopped at 8 p.m., and when he opened it to fix it, the clock started working like before. Then, he thought *how strange, this had never happened before. Tomorrow, I'll ask Mrs. Muller.* After he had picked up all the broken pieces, he went to bed and rested after a long and exciting day.

The following morning, before breakfast, Mrs. Muller went to pick up the broken pieces in the hall area, but she found it all cleaned. She thought Mr. Conrad must have cleaned it the night before and probably taken the *leather bag. I won't either if he doesn't mention it; I hope he is not upset.*

When Conrad came to the kitchen for breakfast, and before Helga could say anything, he gave the news about the new baby boy, and Mrs. Muller and little Lucy reacted so happily that for a moment, the housekeeper forgot what happened the night before, but that didn't last too long, because right after that Conrad asked her about the broken stuff in the hall. Helga hesitated for a moment, and then, she told him, "I heard someone knocking at the door, and when I opened it, no one was there. The wind It was blowing so strongly that a gust came in wide, opening the door, throwing me back inside, and causing all that damage. I got so scared that I closed the door and took Lucy to her room, thinking of cleaning everything the following day. I'm sorry, sir, especially for your beautiful mirror. "

She conveniently didn't mention the female voice or the little man with the leather bag to avoid Conrad thinking she was crazy. Although Helga had been working with the Logans for over five years and used to be Helen's nanny, she didn't have the same rapport with Conrad.

After a short pause, Conrad responded, "Don't worry, Helga. It's only a mirror. The important thing is that you and Lucy are okay." He didn't ask her anything else. Changing the subject, he said, "Lucy, let's go and meet your new brother. Mrs. Muller, get you and Lucy ready. We're going to the hospital to see Helen and the baby."

Later that morning, when they arrived at the hospital, Lucy was so excited to meet her baby brother that Mrs. Muller took her directly to the maternity room window to see the babies; when there, something caught the little girl's attention. A short man, probably no more than our feet tall, dressed in strange clothes, was beside the baby's crib. She immediately asked Mrs. Muller who that man was, but Mrs. Muller couldn't see him and said, "W-what are you talking about? What man?" A little confused, Lucy looked at Mrs. Muller and ran to her father to tell him.

"Daddy, daddy... a little man is standing by the baby! Come quickly, I want to show you!" The nanny lifted her shoulders as if to say, 'I don't know what she's talking about.'

"Sweetie, this isn't the moment to play..." her father said.

"I'm not playing, Daddy; there's a short man with the baby. Come with me and see for yourself!" Helen, who was listening, winked at Conrad and asked him to go with their daughter and see what she meant. Reluctantly, Conrad took Lucy back to the window, and of course, he didn't see anything unusual either, so he told his daughter,

"You see, sweetie, there's no one here. You probably just imagined it!" Since the man wasn't there anymore, the little girl responded,

"Daddy, I saw him; he was right there!" pointing by the baby's crib. Her father, so as not to make her feel bad, said,

"It was probably a little angel taking care of your brother. This is going to be our secret. Okay?"

"Okay, Daddy," Lucy said, smiling at her father.

Mrs. Muller took advantage of Helen's being alone and told her about what happened the night before. Once again, she avoided the part about the strange man. Helen appeared distressed. Helen calmed her down, telling her not to worry and adding, " In most old houses, you always hear strange noises." The old nanny nodded in understanding but couldn't help wondering what she heard and saw that night.

When the baby was taken to the room, Helen showed him to Lucy, who looked at her brother with pride and kissed him tenderly.

******

The following morning, Helen and the baby left the hospital, and on their way home, something odd happened. While stopped at a red light, practically out of nowhere, the same man who gave the leather bag to Mrs. Muller on the night of the baby's birth approached the car, this time dressed differently. He knocked on Conrad's window, pointed at the baby, and gave him a beautiful red rose, so beautiful, it seemed made out of silk. As Conrad passed the rose to Helen, the man whispered,

"FOR OUR LITTLE KEYMASTER…LET THE ROSE PROTECT HIM." And immediately turned back.

Helen was fascinated by the beauty of that rose while the confused Conrad tried to call the man. But he continued walking and suddenly disappeared into the crowd. The light turned green, and Conrad had to go on, so he passed the intersection. He wondered where the man had gone and what his gift meant. Turning to Helen, he asked, "Did you hear what the man said?"

"No, I didn't, but I never saw such a beautiful rose."

Conrad only nodded and said nothing else; neither he nor Helen could imagine the real reason for that beautiful gift or how long it would stay in the family.

When they arrived home, a welcome committee was waiting for them. A giant banner said, "Congratulations, it's a boy," and balloons hung all over the hall and living room. Mrs. Muller, Lucy, Helen's parents, and siblings were all there to receive the new addition to the family. Everyone commented on the beautiful rose Helen had in her hand, and she said it was a gift for the baby. She asked Mrs. Muller to put it in a vase in the baby's room.

Later that night, while everybody was sleeping, the same little man who had been at the hospital before returned to visit the baby. After dropping some magic dust inside the vase holding the rose, he approached the baby and said,

"PLEASANT DREAMS... MY LITTLE MASTER... THE ROSE WILL SEE YOU GROW." and the baby smiled...

Chapter Two: Luscious and Thaddeus

Early the following day, when Helen went to tent the baby, she found something unique; the rose had turned into a little rosebush full of roots. She immediately called Conrad. When he saw it, he lifted his eyebrows and said, "Wow, how is this possible? I've never seen anything like this. Let me take it outside and plant it in the rose garden." He took it and sewed it in the middle of the rose garden, without knowing that he was doing exactly what that little man wanted and without noticing that Chester the puppy was watching him closely.

******

From then on, that rosebush became Helen's favorite. Producing always beautiful roses, especially during the days surrounding Andy's birthdays, when usually roses hardly blossom because of the cold weather.

The first few years of Andy's life were average, as he grew up like any ordinary kid, but everything changed drastically on his seventh birthday.

As he awoke that morning, he found two little men standing by his bed, probably no more than four feet tall. They were dressed in clothes from a fairy tale book and wearing long whiskers. Andy was about to scream when one of the small men covered his mouth and asked him not to yell. Then, they said, "Happy Birthday, Master Andy. Do not be afraid; we are Luscious and Thaddeus and are here to protect you."

Andy was so bewildered as they pointed at each other that he couldn't speak.

"We're dwarves from the realm of Ethernia. You're the only one who can see or hear us… so telling the others about us wouldn't be a good idea because they won't believe you." One of the dwarves added.

At that moment, Lucy, Andy's older sister, entered his room as usual without knocking, this time to say happy birthday to her kid brother, and Andy did precisely what the two little men told him not to do. Pointing at them, he introduced them to his sister. The dwarves looked at him in disbelief and nodded their heads. Since she couldn't see them, she said, "What are you talking about? I don't see anybody here."

"You don't see them? They're right there… look!" Andy pointed at them once again.

"There is no one here. You think I'm stupid?" she yelled.

"You're too big to play with imaginary friends," she finally said, leaving Andy's room.

Young Andy lowered his head in frustration, and the dwarves told him, "We told you she wouldn't see us." …After a sigh, Andy asked them, "How did you get into my room?"

"In time, you'll understand. All you need to know now is that we're your friends, and we came to protect you."

Since that day and for the next thirteen months, they were inseparable, at school, the playground, church… in sum, everywhere... forming a solid bond and, on more than one occasion, getting the boy not only out of danger but out of trouble, especially at school, causing the other students to wonder why he seemed so lucky. What the dwarves didn't realize was that by playing and talking to them, Andy didn't want to play with other children anymore. He always seemed isolated, playing alone and talking to himself. So, one day, his parents, concerned by his behavior and with the advice of his teacher, decided to take him to see a psychologist.

The dwarves didn't want Andy to be treated differently. Like he was crazy, no one would believe him if he told them about them. Therefore, they took the drastic decision to disappear, and one night, just before he went to sleep, they told him,

"Little Master, we don't want people to treat you differently so that we will be invisible to you from now on, too. We'll be nearby, watching you, but you won't be able to see or hear us anymore. We're sorry... this is for your good, Master!"

He immediately replied, "Please don't do that... you're my only friends. Don't go, please!"

Then, they started disappearing, saying, "Goodbye, little master, don't be afraid... Everything is going to be fine." And Andy began crying. He cried for hours until he finally gave up and fell asleep. He cried for many nights until one day, he didn't cry anymore. After more than one year of therapy, he finally convinced himself that, indeed, they were two imaginary friends, and he decided to forget about them.

******

Seven years had passed, and the two little men from Ethernia were only distant dreams in Andy's memory. During his therapy, and to help him gain self-confidence, his parents encouraged him to play sports. Andy chose swimming, which helped him to be quite popular, especially in his school, where he became one of the stars of the swimming team. Academically, he was equally good. His grades were among the highest in his class.

On the night of his fifteenth birthday, just around midnight, when everyone was asleep, a series of unusual events started happening. First, a strange noise like a deep whistle was heard, awakening everyone. Then, a strong wind made the whole house tremble, opening some windows and causing some ornaments and pictures to fall to the floor.

Mrs. Muller came out of her room yelling words in German that no one understood. Andy and Lucy also got up, and Chester, over 15 years old, began acting out of control. Helen and Conrad calmed everyone down and sent them back to their rooms, but they were so scared that they decided to go to the kitchen to have some hot chocolate, one of Mrs. Muller's specialties.

Later, when everyone returned to bed, Andy heard a strange sound coming from outside his room, a female voice humming in a sad tone, like a lament. When he opened the door to see what it was, he noticed no one else had left their room. He was the only one who could hear that voice, which seemed to be coming from the attic. Curious, he put on his robe and quickly saw if the sound was coming from there.

He tried to open the door, but it was locked, and then he remembered one of his father's rules: never go into the attic without telling one of his parents first. It was too late to ask for it, and since the key was in one of the kitchen cabinets, he went directly to the kitchen to fetch it. When he got inside the attic, the sound stopped. He looked over and waited several minutes, but no more sound. Tired of waiting, he returned to bed, wondering why he was the only one who had heard that voice.

Days passed and weeks, but the strange sound was never heard again, and he soon forgot all about it.

******

Since the day the dwarves disappeared on Andy when he was eight years old, he has found a new best friend—Danny McKenzie. Danny lives only a block from Andy and attends the same grade and school. Danny is a friendly, chubby boy, a little clueless at times but highly loyal with a great heart. They have been inseparable for the last few years, sharing many moments, and their respective parents consider them like brothers.

A few weeks before Andy's sixteenth birthday, on Halloween night, to be precise, right after finishing the last trick-or-treating with his pal Danny, Andy came home and was about to receive a big surprise. His parents and Lucy weren't home, and Mrs. Muller had gone to bed early. So, as he was having a drink in the kitchen, someone peculiarly knocked at the back door. Surprised by that knocking, he went to open the door, wondering who would be there. Nothing could prepare him for what he was about to see. Standing by the door were none other than the dwarves Luscious and Thaddeus, who said at once,

"Trick or treat... Master Andy," Andy looked at them in shock with his mouth open, like he was seeing some ghost; his face started turning so pale that he almost fainted. The dwarves had to grab him before he fell. Then, they told him,

"Master, we're back!"

Snapping out of the impression and almost gasping, Andy said, "This isn't possible. You two were a dream...you are not real."

"Master, we're real," Thaddeus responded.

Andy looked at them again, and after a sigh, he started yelling, "**I cried for months. Where have you been all this time?**"

"We're sorry, Master, but we disappeared for your good. Everybody started to believe that you were crazy!"

"**Crazy... Are you kidding me? I went to therapy for years.**"

Andy finally calmed down, and after a long conversation, he reconciled with the two little men. Then he asked them, "Why do you appear now?"

"We are here to prepare you; it's almost your sixteenth birthday. The Gatekeeper is about to unveil the secret of the rose, and then you'll have to become the Keymaster!"

"Wait a second! What do you mean by becoming the Keymaster, and who's the Gatekeeper?" Andy asked, still bewildered.

"Master, you have a clover marked in your left forearm, and the legend says he who's marked by the clover will be the Keymaster of the gate to Ethernia," Thaddeus replied

"I don't understand. What gate? And what's Ethernia?" Andy asked. He had forgotten everything the dwarves told him when he was younger.

"Look at the clover mark on your arm!" Luscious yelled.

Andy pulled his sleeve up and, looking at the birthmark on his left forearm, said, "This is what you meant by the clover?"

"Yes, Master. We'll explain everything soon enough; Ethernia is the land from where we are coming from, and please don't forget that you're the only one who can see us."

Then, pointing at Chester, Thaddeus said, "He's the Gatekeeper!"

"What? My dog, the gatekeeper… the gatekeeper of what?"

"You'll know everything before the next full moon, master. We'll need to watch the gatekeeper and see what he does from now on."

By then, Chester was already a sixteen-year-old dog but looked and acted like a younger dog. The Logans had always taken good care of him but wondered why their beloved dog was still alive and unusually healthy for his age.

******

One week before his birthday, Andy was coming from Danny's house. As he opened the back door, Chester ran to him and started acting very hyper, wagging his tail rapidly and jumping all over, as if trying to tell him something. Andy bent down and kissed him. The dog grabbed Andy by his pants and pulled him outside to the backyard.

Andy didn't understand what was happening and said, "Chester, stop! Don't do that. You're hurting me!"

Chester released Andy, ran to the rose garden, and began digging in the middle. Andy tried to stop him, but the dwarves appeared and said, "Let him master. It is time… the moon is full!"

Andy and the dwarves moved closer to see what the dog was digging. At that moment, Chester pulled a leather bag from that hole and gave it to a confused Andy, who couldn't understand what was happening. Then Thaddeus told him, "It's all right, master. Open it!"

Using extreme caution, Andy opened the bag and pulled out a small black box and a piece of folded paper. Looking at his dog, he said, "So this is what you've been protecting all these years."

Chester was always very protective of the rose garden, letting no one near it but Helen. Now Andy understood why. He approached his dog, grabbed his head, and said, "Very clever boy… good boy!" and kissed him.

Andy quickly covered the hole made by Chester and returned to the house; Mrs. Muller, who was in the kitchen, saw through the window what was happening in the garden. Andy hid the little package, but a little too late, then she asked him, in her usual heavy accent and stammering,

"W-what are you hiding, Andy, and what were you and Chester doing in the rose garden?"

"Nothing, Mrs. Muller. I was playing with Chester, that's all."

Mrs. Muller knew Andy so well that she didn't believe him, and she asked him again what he was hiding. However, he insisted it was nothing, so she decided not to ask him anymore. Chester went to his bed, and Andy ran to his room, followed by his two little friends. After he locked the door, he unfolded the paper; it was a note that read,

TO THE KEYMASTER ON HIS SIXTEENTH BIRTHDAY… NOW IS THE TIME TO OPEN THE GATE!

Turning back the paper, he found the following riddle:

When the sky stops crying and the moon smiles, find the singing rose. She will sing the magic words and release the golden key. Find the music box, look over the dancing couple, and read the instructions at the top; then, you'll know how to open the gate and follow your dreams.

Andy looked at the two dwarves, not knowing what to say, and then Thaddeus said, "Master Andy, you'll need to solve this riddle so you can open the gate to Ethernia!"

"Yeah, and how will I be able to do that?" He replied, a little discouraged, but after a sigh, he added, "I have to resolve this riddle before my birthday. It looks like there's a key inside this box, and I need to find another box with the dancing couple… and read something there to make that gate appear. It sounds tricky but not impossible," he said.

"Don't you worry, Master, we'll help you!" Thaddeus said.

"Okay," Andy replied, and after a few words of encouragement from the dwarves, they said goodbye and left for the day.

Later that night, when Andy went to bed, he took longer than usual to fall asleep, thinking about everything that had happened that day, the little black box found in the rose garden, the mysterious riddle, and what was coming for him…

Chapter Three: The Sixteenth Birthday

The following day, on their way to school, Andy finally dared to share his secret his with Danny, so after begging him not to laugh or think he was crazy, he started telling him about the noises coming from his attic and that he was the only one who could hear, about the finding of a black box hiding in his mother's rose garden by his dog Chester, about the meaning of his peculiar birthmark and finally about his two little friends, the dwarves from Ethernia. After he finished telling his story, Danny looked at him without saying a single word; he seemed confused but also fascinated at the same time, so after a few endless seconds, Danny gave a big sigh and said,

"Dude, you're my best friend, a little crazy, but my friend. I'm in… What can I do?" He accepted every word his friend said; his loyalty to Andy was unconditional.

"I was afraid you would think I'm crazy, but I knew you were the only one who could believe me. Thanks, Danny!"

Over the following days, they spent most of their time together trying to solve the riddle, and Andy told Danny about his relationship with the dwarves. There were only a few days before Andy's birthday, and they were against the clock. So far, they have resolved the first part of the riddle.

"When the sky stopped crying, it meant it would be raining that day, and we would have to wait for it to stop." Andy said, then he added, "The moon is smiling."

"It had to be referring to one of the moon's phases (the new moon that looks like a smile, also called the Cheshire moon.)"

"See the singing rose? We probably will find it in the rose garden. The rest was a little bit more complicated. We'll have to wait for the rose to release the golden key, which will give us some clue where to look for the music box. I'm sure my little friends will help me with that," he said.

With each day passing, Danny became more and more convinced that the dwarves were for real; he even dared to address them on a few occasions, which looked very funny because he usually ended up talking to himself. Meanwhile, Andy asked the dwarves the same question: Where can you find that music box? They kindly gave him the same response: "Sorry, Master… we can't tell you anything until your birthday. The golden key has to be released first!"

In the early hours of his 16th birthday, it was still dark when Andy abruptly awoke and was disturbed; the dwarves, watching over him, immediately asked Andy why he awoke like that, and he said, "I had a strange dream. I was running on a narrow road, chased by some monster; then I saw a castle at the end of the road, but as I got closer, the castle seemed to move farther away. Thaddeus told them, "Master, don't trouble yourself. It's only a bad dream. Try to get some sleep. You need it." And then, without Andy noticing, they sprinkled some magic dust over his head, and he fell asleep for the rest of the night.

In the morning, when Andy awoke, the dwarves were the first to greet him. "Happy sixteenth birthday, master…we wish your life full of good things…now, we have to prepare everything for tonight, so we'll see you later. Have a great day…Aah! Don't forget to get the magnifying glass."

"What for?" Andy asked. Thaddeus responded as they were disappearing. "To read the inscription in the box."

It was still early; everyone was still in bed except Mrs. Muller, who was preparing Andy's favorite breakfast in the kitchen. Taking advantage of that, Andy left his room and quickly went to his father's office to take the magnifying glass, returning immediately to his room without being noticed. When there, he sat on his bed, and suddenly everything came back to him like a cold shower, and he started to feel anxious and preoccupied with what was about to happen later that day. Fortunately for him, only a few minutes later, his parents came into his room singing Happy Birthday. That was all Andy needed to feel more relaxed, and then the three of them went down to the kitchen to see what Mrs. Muller was fixing for breakfast.

When the family finished breakfast, Andy opened the presents his parents and Mrs. Muller gave him; the old housekeeper/nanny gave him a nice lotion and his parents a small box, which he opened, finding a set of keys, he looked at them, and then they told him to go to the garage. There, he found a nice electric bike. He thanked his parents with a big hug, and then he returned to his room to get ready for the party scheduled for that afternoon and, most importantly, for the big challenge of the night: solving the riddle and opening the black box.

Of course, his pal Danny was the first to arrive around noon. He came right when the birthday boy got out of the shower, helping him relax and prepare for the party.

About one hour later, someone knocked at Andy's door; it was Grandpa Donovan who opened the door and said,

"Well, my dear boy, happy birthday. You're a fine young man now. Your mother told me about your interest in riddles and their meaning. So, I have the perfect gift for you!"

"Hi Grandpa, it's so good to see you!"

Grandpa Donovan gave Andy a present, which he immediately opened. It was a book about old sayings and riddles. Then Grandpa added,

"Come down, my dear boy. Your grandmother wants to hug you and has an envelope for you!"

"Okay, Grandpa. I'll be down in a minute!" Andy waited until Grandpa had left the room, and he said to Danny, "This gift couldn't be more appropriate, don't you think?"

"You bet," Danny responded.

Andy came down to salute Grandma Gertrude and welcome other family members and guests. By then, his father was already working on the grill, and Helen and Mrs. Muller were finishing the salads and Andy's favorite dish, potato soufflé with bacon.

It was a lovely day in late November. The temperature was in the upper fifties, with plenty of sunshine, allowing everyone to enjoy the party in the beautiful backyard of the Logan estate. They organized several games to entertain Andy's friends and guests, which helped him get distracted for a few hours, forgetting what he was about to face later that night.

However, right after sunset, the weather changed drastically. The wind began to blow, and distant thunder rumbled, announcing the impending rain. That was the signal for the party to come to an end. About half an hour later, most of the guests had already left. Everyone, including Danny and the grandparents, helped to clean up the mess. Then, the weather worsened, and the first raindrops began to fall.

Suddenly, a strange phenomenon caught Andy's attention. Although the wind was moving bushes and trees, the rose garden seemed calm, and no rain was falling there. Stunned by the view, he pulled Danny over to show him the strange thing. It didn't occur to either of them that the dwarves were responsible for protecting that area from the storm.

The rain started falling harder, so Conrad called everybody inside. By then, the cleaning was practically done, and to keep the party in the same mood, Helen asked Andy to open his presents.

Andy and Danny were still talking about what they had just seen in the rose garden; they didn't notice that Lucy had not only seen it but also when Andy showed it to Danny. A little confused, she started thinking,

These guys are looking at that… Andy has been acting strangely lately, so I'd better keep an eye on him.

Andy began to open his presents, and almost immediately, one of them grabbed his attention. It was a small box looking like a pentagon, wrapped in green paper and tied with a golden bow. It had a little note on it. He grabbed the box, noticing immediately that the handwriting was very peculiar, probably from somebody who had not shown up at the party. Somebody from the same place as his friends, the dwarves, comes from.

Helen and Mrs. Muller were serving hot chocolate and cake, so taking advantage of everyone's distraction, he quickly hid the present inside one of the other present bags and winked at Danny, who didn't notice the move, looked clueless, and said, "What?"

At the stroke of 8:00 pm, right after Andy had opened the last present, the large window in the middle of the stairs flew open with a burst of wind, and the mirror in front of it fell, shattering into many pieces. Then, a strange cry, like a mournful wail, scared everyone there, especially Mrs. Muller.

Conrad ran to see what had happened. He called the guys to help him close the large window. The beautiful mirror was now lying on the floor, shattered. Conrad looked sad because that mirror had been in the family for at least three generations.

After closing the window, they swiped up the broken mirror pieces, and everyone returned to the family room. By then, Lucy began wondering if any of these events were related to what she had seen before. She couldn't imagine that she would discover the truth later that night.

After Andy's uncles and grandparents left, Andy asked Danny to help him take the presents to his room; Danny immediately grabbed some of the bags and followed Andy to his room. When they were there, they quickly closed the door, and as expected, Andy opened the mysterious gift first. It was a small box in the shape of a pentagon. Inside, he found a little bottle filled with golden dust and a note that read?

"Use the golden dust to beat the final task."

Andy remained silent while Danny asked, "What's that dude?"

"I don't know, but I'd better put this away. I'm sure it's important."

When the rain stopped, Danny left, not before saying to Andy, "I want full disclosure, ok." Andy nodded and then said goodbye to his best friend.

It was minutes after 9:30 p.m., so everyone retired to their rooms. Andy changed into his pajamas and waited patiently for his chance to go to the rose garden. His parents came to say goodnight, and he thought, "I'll wait till they close their door… I'll be ready."

There was distant thunder. Andy knew he didn't have much time before the rain started again, but he needed to wait until his parents closed their bedroom door.

Right at the stroke of 10:00 p.m., Andy's father finally closed his bedroom door, so Andy said to himself. "I've got to go now before the rain starts again."

He put on his robe and grabbed a flashlight and the magnifying glass. Then he took the leather bag from his nightstand, put it inside his pocket, and left his room…

Chapter Four: The Secret Place

As he opened the door, his two friends from Ethernia showed up. Andy almost screamed, forcing Luscious to cover the boy's mouth. Andy breathed profoundly and whispered, "Oh my God, you scared me to death! I almost screwed up everything. Where have you two been the whole day?!"

"Sorry, Master," the dwarves replied at the same time. Then Thaddeus added, "We had been preparing everything for tonight, master. Also, we protected the rose garden during the storm."

"Please don't show up like this again," Andy asked them.

"Master, we promise to announce ourselves next time!" Luscious replied.

"Before we go down, I want to tell you something," Andy said. Then he added, "I received a strange present, a little bottle with golden dust…" And Thaddeus responded, "That's a gift from Fedora. You'll need it in your final task."

"Perfect! Who is Fedora, and what will be my final task?"

"Fedora is the Queen of the lake, and no one knows your final task yet. The oracle told her to prepare that for you. You'll know more later; now the singing rose is waiting, Master," Thaddeus answered.

"Right… the singing Rose." Andy sarcastically said, then added, "Let's go before the rain starts again. We must be careful when we pass my parents' bedroom to avoid disturbing them. They could be awake; their TV is still on."

Then, Luscious quickly responded, "Don't worry, Master. They are sleeping like logs; they won't wake up, even with an earthquake!"

"So, I guess every second counts!" Andy said as he and the dwarves were leaving his room. Seconds later, they passed by Conrad and Helen's bedroom so focused that they forgot to check on Lucy. They assumed she was sleeping, too, since her door was closed and her lights were out. But as they were taking the stairs down, she opened her door slightly and saw Andy coming down, talking to himself, so she grabbed her robe and followed him.

When they got to the backyard, Luscious turned his head and told Thaddeus, "I felt something. Let me go back and check." Thaddeus nodded and then continued walking with Andy toward the rose garden.

The new moon was brilliant and looked like a big smile, illuminating the rose garden. The center featured Helen's rosebush with a beautiful red rose swinging nicely in the wind, producing a humming-like sound. Then Andy said, "That must be the singing rose."

At that moment, Lucy opened the door from the kitchen to the backyard and started to go the few steps down to get to the backyard, very slowly, not to give herself away, but then she was spooked by Luscious, who appeared behind her, pulled her robe, saying: "…Boo!"

She could hardly contain her scream and almost fainted. Then Luscious told her, "Shame on you, Lady Lucy, following us like this…"

Lucy, utterly surprised, looked at the little man and exclaimed, "Oh my God…who are you? And what are you doing here?"

"My name is Luscious, and I am from Ethernia. We're here to protect your brother, Andy. However, this is a long story, and I don't have time to explain it now. You'll have to trust me and come with us now… but don't say anything. We'll explain everything later!"

"What are you talking about? What is Ethernia? Tell me now, or I'll scream and call my parents!"

"Are you sure you want to do that? We can disappear again, and it'll be hard to explain what you're doing here at this hour."

Luscious didn't want to tell her that her parents wouldn't wake up even if a bomb went off. Lucy hesitated and, realizing that the dwarf was right, answered. "Okay, but I want to know everything… Do you understand?"

"Fair enough, my lady," Luscious replied.

Andy and Thaddeus were already in the rose garden, closer to the singing rose, when Luscious and Lucy came right behind them,

"Master Andy, wait up!" Luscious exclaimed.

Andy turned, and when he saw his sister, he reacted as though he was looking at the ghost of Christmas future. For a few seconds, he remained speechless with his mouth open. On the contrary, Lucy asked him without hesitation,

"What are you doing here, and who are these people?"

Like a stroke of lightning, Andy replied, "Never mind who these men are. I'll explain things later. We don't have a moment to lose now!"

Impressed by her brother's tone, Lucy remained silent while Andy took the leather bag out of his pocket, pulled the little box, and, standing in front of the rose, asked the dwarves, "Now, what am I supposed to do?"

Luscious answered, "Be patient, Master; the rose will tell you what to do. It should be a few more seconds. Now, please look at the moon."

At that moment, the moonlight was touching directly on the rose, which looked more beautiful than ever. Andy pulled back one step when suddenly the rose started to whisper the following:

"Oh, little box... let me touch you with my petals to break the seal and release the golden key."

A little confused, Andy yelled at the dwarves, "Guys, what did she say?"

Thaddeus yelled, "Let the rose touch the box!"

Andy began to bring the box closer and closer to the rose. When it finally touched its petals, the rose stopped singing. Two seconds later, the rose said, *"Lord Keymaster... let the key make you worthy."*

The box fell from Andy's hand and opened just before it hit the ground. A gorgeous golden key, no bigger than a pinky, fell out. Then, all of the petals of the singing rose dropped to the ground, and a powerful sound of thunder was heard, signaling that the rain was about to start again.

Luscious told Andy, "Master, get the key. Now we need to find the dancing couple in the secret place. Let's go!"

Andy hastily picked up the key and said, "My mother isn't going to like this in the morning. These are her favorite roses. Where are we going now?"

"Back to the house. We need to go to the secret place!"

Lucy, who had been watching everything until then but had no clue what was happening, asked, "What's going on here? What's the secret place?"

Andy responded, "Lucy, shut up and come with us!"

Lucy didn't like Andy's tone and responded, "My dear brother, I'm involved now, so you better tell me what's going on before I tell Mom and Dad, okay?"

Then, Thaddeus interrupted in a low but firm tone, "I'll explain everything, Lady Lucy. All you need to know is that you're very much involved in this story; now you can see us too, meaning, although we don't know how, you'll have to help, too, like Master Andy!"

"What do you say?" she yelled.

Thaddeus grabbed her hand and took her inside the house. After they sat on one of the living room couches, he started explaining everything at such a fast pace. It was terrific how Lucy was listening and understanding simultaneously; it seemed like magic.

When Luscious and Andy were inside the house, Andy asked him, "What's the secret place?"

"It's the room at the end of the hall on the second floor."

"I knew it! Andy exclaimed. "I knew something was happening in the attic; strange things have been occurring there for years."

After picking up the attic key from the cabinet in the kitchen, Andy and Luscious went upstairs. Andy signaled to Luscious to stay silent. He didn't want Mrs. Muller to wake up. Luscious told him, "Don't worry about the nice old lady. She's also sleeping like a rock."

Andy chuckled, and when they passed by his parents' room, he opened the door and looked inside. His parents were both in deep sleep. It seemed as though they were enchanted (which they were). Andy asked, "They look frozen. Are you sure they are fine?"

"Of course, they are, Master," Luscious stated.

A few steps back, Lucy and Thaddeus were getting closer, and Lucy whispered, "Guys, wait up!"

A few seconds later, they stood in front of the attic door. Andy inserted the key and opened it slowly. When they got inside, a female voice started to hum a beautiful melody, and they looked at each other in surprise. Then the rain started again, and the thunderclaps were so strong that the electricity went off briefly. This caused absolute darkness in the attic. Andy automatically turned on his flashlight, and the confused Lucy said, "Where's that voice coming from?"

"That's what we have to find out," Andy responded.

Then, they saw something that caught their attention. A red shade in the form of a clover was flashing on the bottom of a pile of boxes in one of the corners.

"Right there in that corner!" Andy said.

Curious to see what was inside the box, Lucy was the first to help, moving some boxes on top of the marked one, which was covered by a gray blanket. Then, the clover mark disappeared, and the electricity came back on. The female voice was coming from under that blanket.

Andy didn't recall seeing that blanket before, but he never paid too much attention to the attic. When they removed the blanket, they found a black metal chest with golden borders. It was in such a good state that it was difficult to determine its age.

Andy sighed and slowly lifted the top of the chest to reveal a gorgeous wooden box. It was made of the finest carved oak and had a solid gold dragon's head on top. Very carefully, Andy pulled the box out of the chest and placed it on top of the only table in the attic.

The two little men's anxiety was growing. After a pause, Andy looked at Lucy, who exclaimed, "Open it, Andy!"

Andy pulled out the golden key and unlocked the wooden box. At that moment, a gentle breeze came through the small window, and everyone felt uneasy. Andy lifted the top, unveiling a delicate music box. It looked so beautiful that everyone's eyes shone at the sight of it.

In the center were two porcelain figurines of a dancing couple, so perfectly made that they looked almost real. They were facing each other as if they were ready to start dancing. On the inside top was a small mirror surrounded by precious gems, featuring a rare inscription. The mechanism was located on the right side of the figurines, featuring a winding key made of gold.

Completely fascinated by the music box, Lucy whispered, "Wow! It's so beautiful. I've never seen anything like this."

Andy and Lucy gazed at this marvelous art piece without knowing the secret hidden there…

Chapter Five: The Enchanted Couple

The siblings remained speechless for a few more seconds, and then, Andy was the first to break the silence; almost whispering, he said, "Oh my God! How perfect! They look like real people!"

"And they are, Master… They are!" Luscious blurted out.

Andy and Lucy looked at each other, wide-eyed, and then Thaddeus explained, "You're looking at Princess Morgana of Ambrosia and Prince Nolan of Utopia. The evil and powerful Zoltar enchanted them into this box. They were chosen to consolidate the peace in Ethernia and bring harmony and happiness for many years. Zoltar got them just before their wedding, breaking the perfect balance in the land and bringing evil, fear, and darkness. Since then, he became the usurper and ruler of Ethernia."

"Give me a break… that's impossible!" Lucy remarked in disbelief, looking at the surprised Thaddeus.

"Don't interrupt, Lucy!" a disturbed Andy said, and then he added, "Forgive my sister, Thaddeus, and please tell us more."

"No problem, Master, but it's a long story…"

"We have plenty of time, Thaddeus. Besides, I want to know what this story has to do with me and why you guys are calling me the Keymaster. So, my friend, we're all ears."

"I'm sorry for the interruption," Lucy said, a little embarrassed. Then, looking at her brother, she added, "You're right, Andy... I want to know, too."

Everyone was so fascinated with the music box that they momentarily forgot something important. Andy suddenly remembered and said, "Wait, Thaddeus. What about the inscription we have to read?"

Pointing at the box, Thaddeus said, "You're right, master. It's that little one over the mirror, but you'll need a magnifying glass to read it." Andy pulled the one he took from his father's office and, approaching the box, pointed his flashlight and read:

FULL MOON WILL HAVE TO BE, TO USE THE GOLDEN KEY... LET THE MOONLIGHT TOUCH THE BOX AND READ TWICE THE MAGIC WORDS. THE GOLDEN GATE WILL COME... AND YOU WILL ENTER OUR LAND TO FACE YOUR DESTINY...

Andy looked at the dwarves, like saying, "Now what?"

Thaddeus immediately said, "Master, it means you'll have to wait until the next full moon to open the gate to Ethernia. You'll have to go there to meet your first task, which I'm sure we'll know before then. Now, let me tell you the story." Andy nodded in understanding, and Thaddeus continued.

"Many years ago, in the beautiful and peaceful realm of Ethernia, also known as the land of the eternal spring. The neighboring kingdoms of Ambrosia and Utopia were about to celebrate their five hundred years of peace, but according to an old prophecy, the kingdoms would face an evil threat. By that time, the planets were about to align, giving the dark wizard Zoltar, frozen in eternal sleep inside a cell in the forbidden mountain, enough power to awake, bringing great danger to the land. Only a strong union between the two kingdoms before the alignment would protect them from that terrible prophecy.

As I mentioned before, Ethernia was a paradise. The weather was always perfect, the flowers bloomed all year round, and the birds were always singing. Some mornings after a soft rain, the rainbow would show the way between the two kingdoms, separated by the emerald forest. On the south side of the forest, we have the forbidden mountains, named like that because it was forbidden for any man or dwarf in the whole realm to disturb them; the dark wizard Zoltar was imprisoned there. Both kingdoms had a garrison of soldiers posted at the bottom with orders not to let anyone pass.

King Noble of Ambrosia and King Percival of Utopia arranged a royal wedding to guarantee a strong union. This wedding was initially agreed upon about a decade before, when Noble visited Percival on the occasion of his twenty-five years on the throne. Prince Nolan was twelve years old, and Princess Morgana was only nine. At that time, they didn't like each other and swore never to marry, even if they were the last people on the land.

Thus, everyone in Ethernia was getting ready for the big event. Even the dwarves of the Emerald Forest were invited to participate. The exceptions were the Prince and the Princess. They couldn't bear watching the preparations for a wedding they didn't want to attend. But it was their duty to fulfill this engagement for the sake of the Realm.

Two weeks before the wedding, Morgana went to the Dwarf Village, located in Emerald Forest, to visit her best friend Lumi, the daughter of the dwarf chief. She always found peace there, and she needed that before making what she believed would be the most significant sacrifice of her life.

At the same time, Prince Nolan, a passionate hunter, also went to the forest. He wanted to keep his mind busy before the wedding, and on that day, for no particular reason, he decided to go deep into the forest, an unfamiliar area for him.

Morgana and Lumi were swimming in Crystal Lake when Nolan, who was only a few hundred yards away, started to follow a magnificent deer. His servant, Basile, warned him not to go too deep into the forest, and the prince said,

'Don't you worry, Basile, I'll be fine. That's the most beautiful deer I've ever seen in my life… Wait here, I'll be back soon.'

By then, Morgana and Lumi were having a conversation about the wedding.

'Lumi, what should I do? I'm about to marry a man I hate, and I'm sure he hates me, too.' The princess said,

'What can I say, my lady? That's your father's will and is for the good of the realm. On the other hand, I know it'll make you miserable, but you have to find the courage to do it. Your duty as a Princess is to put your kingdom before your welfare.'

'Oh, Lumi, what I'd give to be free of this engagement and be able to make my own decisions and control my future.'

Suddenly, the deer stopped by the lake to drink water, only a few yards from where the two young ladies were swimming.

Nolan was getting closer and had a good view of his prey. Without hesitation, he pulled an arrow from his case and aimed it at the magnificent beast when a sweet voice told him, 'No, sir, please don't kill the deer. I beg you!'

Nolan immediately turned to see where that voice was coming from as the deer ran away from the scene. He got closer to the lake, looking for that voice, and then he found the most beautiful girl he had ever seen. She seemed like a mermaid. Her skin was as white as snow, and her light brown hair and blue eyes complemented the color of the water perfectly. She looked at him with gratitude for not killing that magnificent beast and said, 'Thank you, Sir.'

Nolan responded. 'Who are you, and why do you want to save that deer? Are you the lady of these lands?'

'No, sir, I'm a stranger in this land. I'm the guest of Lady Lumi, daughter of Lord Nikos, Chief of the dwarves.'

'Your beauty is beyond anything I've ever seen. May I have your name, please?'

'Sir, we haven't been properly introduced, and I have to leave now... so, I'd kindly appreciate it if you turn around and let me get out of the water.'

'As you wish, my lady, but I must know your name.'

Morgana didn't say anything else and quickly got out of the water along with Lumi, disappearing almost immediately, using the short passage back to the Dwarf Village. When Nolan turned around, nobody was there. Like a mirage, the beautiful lady had vanished. He looked all over the place but couldn't find her anywhere.

Not sure if what he saw was real, he returned to Basile, his loyal servant. Visibly disappointed, he constantly repeated to himself, 'I have to find her; somehow, I have to find her.'

Meanwhile, Morgana hurried back to the dwarf's village, telling Lumi,

'Did you see that knight? He's very handsome! He has a beautiful smile, and his eyes... ohh...I couldn't resist the way he was looking at me.'

'Morgana, you shouldn't talk like that! You're marrying Prince Nolan in two weeks.'

'I hate that man!' Morgana replied, very upset.

'If your father hears you talking like this, he'll be upset, my lady.'

'It's all right, Lumi, I won't say a word, but... you can't deny how handsome he is!'

'That's true, my lady, he's very handsome, but you should erase him from your mind.'

When Nolan finally reached Basile, he was walking distracted, like he was in shock.

'Master, what's bothering you? Talk to me. What's wrong?' Basile asked him,

'You won't believe this, but I just saw the most beautiful girl in the realm; I must find her, Basile. I never saw such beauty and kindness in my life!'

'What are you talking about, sir? You'll go to Ambrosia in less than two weeks to marry Princess Morgana.'

'Please, Basile, don't remind me that… life doesn't make sense. How ironic! I met the woman of my life only weeks before my marriage to another one whom I hate!'

'Well, Master, be reasonable, and don't let your heart deceive you. Remember that your country needs you.'

'I know, Basile, but I'd rather not be a prince and give up everything. I want to be free and choose the woman I love!'

'Master, I heard that Princess Morgana is a beautiful woman.'

'I don't care how beautiful she is. All I know is that I can't get that girl out of my mind!'

'Tomorrow will be another day, and you'll see things differently, Master. Let's go back to the castle…'

'Okay, my loyal friend, let's go!'

******

On the far side of the dwarf village, a small figure dressed all in black was preparing himself for an extraordinary journey. A journey that would take him to the forbidden mountains with only one purpose: to help free the dark wizard.

It was Simon the Dwarf druid, who had been secretly practicing rituals involving black magic and becoming Zoltar's most loyal follower since he had found Zoltar's book years before. He had been waiting for the right time to help his master. Not even Nikos, the chief of the dwarves, had a clue about these secret rituals and how powerful Simon had become.

It was only two weeks before the wedding, and both kingdoms took every precaution not to let anyone pass through the forbidden mountains. They doubled the number of soldiers at the entrance, closed every possible passage, and sent patrols to check the area several times during the day.

Nolan and Basile returned to the castle the next morning; the prince spent the rest of that day very quietly, alone in his chambers, thinking about what happened in the forest. That night during dinner, he didn't say too much when his father asked him about his time hunting. King Percival knew how Nolan felt about this wedding, but also knew he would do his duty for the sake of the realm.

One week later, right after dinner on the night before the journey to Ambrosia, Nolan had a conversation with his father. He tried to get out of the engagement, and the king told him,

'My son, you know perfectly well that you must save your people; you must do what is best for Utopia… not what is best for you.'

'I understand, Father. I won't disappoint you or our people!' Nolan finally retorted.

By then, back in Ambrosia, Morgana felt so miserable that she didn't want to see or talk to anybody except Lumi, her closest friend, who was there keeping her company.

What an irony! Nolan and Morgana were miserable, thinking they would have to make a big sacrifice, without knowing they were about to marry their true loves…"

Chapter Six: The Last Journey

Thaddeus stopped, and when he saw Andy yawning, he said. "Master, are you alright?"

"Yeah, I'm, don't worry about me. I'm a little tired, that's all; let's continue the story." The boy responded

"Are you sure, Master? After all, it has been a long day."

"Please continue, I'll be fine," Andy insisted.

"As you wish, master," Thaddeus replied and then continued.

"That same night in the forest, Simon the dwarf druid, who by then knew many spells from Zoltar's magic book, was waiting for the right time to use the "animalikus spell" to transform himself into a raccoon. That way, he would sneak through the soldiers' camp and search for his Master's cell in the mountains.

Simon's chance came right after midnight, when everyone in the camp was asleep, and a few guards were on watch. He transformed into a raccoon and passed through the garrison's camp quickly. Simon climbed the mountain the whole night and transformed back into himself right at the break of daylight. He had been practicing dark magic since he found Zoltar's book, but without knowing that the power of that book had been controlling him more and more and had given him the task of awakening his master after five hundred years in prison.

That morning, King Percival and the Utopian delegation gathered in the main hall of the castle, and after a few words from his majesty, they started their journey to Ambrosia. Everyone was very excited about the upcoming events; the exception, of course, was Nolan. He was riding very quietly… like a prisoner who was about to be hanged.

The Utopians' first stop would be the Emerald Forest. They wanted to arrive before dark and spend the night closer to Crystal Lake.

******

Meanwhile, at the forbidden mountain, Simon finally reached the darkest side, the cavern marked by the dragon—the one leading to Zoltar's cell. When he entered, the first thing he did was to make Zoltar's book appear. Right after that, a strange voice in dragon language started whispering to him, directing the dwarf through caves and tunnels to the exact location of his master's cell.

It was so dark that he had to light a torch. Giant Rats and snakes protected the place, and it was almost impossible for anybody to get through without being attacked by them. The strange voice ordered the animals to clear a path for the dwarf to pass. As Simon got closer and closer, the voice started repeating.

'ZAKHARA ZOLTAR, ZAKHARA ZOLTAR,' that means' *Wake up, Zoltar 'in dragon's* language.

Simon was getting deeper and deeper into the cave until he stopped in front of a large metal door with strange symbols all around and, in the middle, a magnificent dragon's head. He could translate those symbols with the help of Zoltar's book.

Thus, Simon touched the head of the dragon with his right hand and read the following phrase from the book:

'ZAKHARA ZOLTAR, TU EST LIBERATES…ZAKHARA ZOLTAR, PLANETUS ORDERS PER SUMOM, ZAKHARA ZOLTAR, EFFECTUS.'

Then the metal door began to open slowly, and he saw a shadow standing inside… It was the dark wizard Zoltar, who was still weak but very much awake. Simon came inside and told him, 'Master, finally… you are free!'

Zoltar knew Simon was coming through his connection with his book, and he responded almost panting, 'Good work, Simon, good work…'

******

By then, the Utopians were getting closer to Crystal Lake when a sudden roar came from the mountains. It felt like a small earthquake, but so loud that it could be heard throughout the entire realm. After the commotion, the Utopians started camping without imagining what had caused that terrible sound.

A few miles away at the dwarf village, Nikos, the Dwarf Lord, was extremely worried about that noise. He immediately called for Simon but felt terrible when he found out his wizard was not in the village and had been missing for a few days."

The following day, the Utopians, still confused by what had happened the previous night, gathered together to continue their journey. Nolan was disturbed because he had a bad dream. Basile, who knew him well, asked,

'Why are you looking so distressed, my master?'

'Last night, I had a strange dream, Basile. I was dancing in a dark room with a girl, but I couldn't see her face! All I could hear was her crying. Then, when I tried to separate her from me, I couldn't do it. All I could hear was the soft music and her crying!'

'Don't pay attention, Master; it's only a dream. Don't let that bother you.'

'I don't know, but I have a bad feeling, Basile… it felt so real; I think it was some kind of a message.'

'Please, Your Highness, don't be so negative.'

'Okay, my loyal friend, I'll try to free my mind of these negative thoughts.'

After lifting the camp, the journey was immediately resumed, but a few hours later, the Utopians suffered their first setback. Suddenly, the sky was shrouded in dark clouds, and a powerful storm struck the forest. It never rained like that before, nor at this time of the year, but that day, it seemed like everything was possible. They couldn't advance, so they tried to protect themselves behind some trees.

They couldn't imagine that Zoltar, although still weak, had caused that storm by sending it from his cell at the Forbidden Mountain, trying to delay the Utopians so they wouldn't arrive at Ambrosia on time.

******

At Ambrosia, many people were working in preparation for the festivities. The atmosphere was full of excitement, but the only person in a different mood was Princess Morgana, who was constantly crying and thinking about the mysterious knight she had met at the lake. She couldn't take him out of her mind.

Only her best friend, Lumi, and Alina, her loyal servant, knew what was happening to her. They told her the wedding was necessary to save Ethernia from the terrible prophecy. Words were not enough to make her feel better. Knowing that the Utopian delegation was already going to Ambrosia made her feel worse.

Meanwhile, in the forest, the Utopians were forced not only to travel the whole night to make up for the time they had lost due to the storm but also to cross the darkest part of the forest, where most of the unpleasant and dangerous creatures lived.

The following day, just before dawn, when the Utopians were crossing the dark part of the forest, Zoltar sent them another spell – this time, he sent hundreds of giant bats, almost the size of eagles, to attack them. When the Utopians saw the cloud of bats coming their way, they quickly gathered together in the center, forming a square. They use their shields first to protect Lady Henrietta, the king's sister, and to cover themselves. The bats attacked them in waves that seemed endless. Still, thanks to their skills as archers and swordsmen, the Utopians resisted those attacks again and again, killing many of the bats but losing a few warriors, who died horribly, bitten to death by those horrible creatures. The Utopians were tired but fought magnificently until the few remaining bats disappeared. When the battle ended, there were dead bats all over the ground. Every Utopian, including the king, had blood on his clothes. Thus, after burying their casualties, the Utopians regrouped and continued their journey without realizing that Zoltar was behind the attack. They thought the bats had come from the surrounding caves in the forest.

By sunset, the Utopians arrived at the other end of the forest; they all looked tired, but their spirits were lifted when they saw the beautiful shire of the Valley of Ambrosia, a magnificent landscape of meadows and small hills, all covered by the greenest grass ever seen. The sides of the road were filled with colorful flowers and beautiful trees. The river ran not far from the road, and the sun was beginning to set just behind it. It looked like a painting of a beautiful and peaceful landscape. King Percival ordered them to stop and camp by the river, where they spent the night. They were only a few hours away from the city of Ambrosia. Thus, after the first peaceful night in three days, the Utopians had the chance to rest well.

The well-rested utopians started the last part of their journey the following day. Their mood was more relaxed, and their excitement was increasing. Even Nolan was a little more cheerful and told Basile,

'Well, my loyal friend... this is the day!'

'That's the attitude, Master. I'm sure you'll like Princess Morgana; Rumors said her beauty doesn't compare!'

'I hear that she's a spoiled brat who got everything she wanted!' Nolan exclaimed.

'Master, at least give her a chance!'

'Let's go and get over with it, my friend.'

'Good for you, Master!' Basile finally said.

Early that afternoon, the Utopians were finally at the entrance of Ambrosia city, where a committee led by Lord Pendleton (head of Ambrosia's army) welcomed them to their city.

After the protocol, the visitors followed Lord Pendleton to the royal castle. The people cheered them as they passed through the city, throwing flowers and confetti; the hurrahs were heard around town. Lord Pendleton informed King Percival that King Noble and Queen Lydia were waiting for them in the castle to offer a welcoming toast and attend a banquet; a masked ball had been organized to introduce Princess Morgana to Prince Nolan. Henrietta, sister of King Percival, who was riding by his brother's side, was thrilled with that idea.

When the visitors arrived at the castle, Alina, the servant, was at the window looking at the Utopian delegation and immediately told Morgana, 'My lady, come and look; the Utopians are arriving.'

'I don't want to see anybody.'

'Oh, but the prince looks very handsome, my lady!'

'I don't want to see that arrogant jerk,' Morgana retorted.

Then, the Utopian delegation was received by the king and queen with a welcome banquet, after which they were taken to their rooms to prepare for the masquerade."

******

Andy and Lucy followed the story with such attention back in the attic, and their interest increased with every word Thaddeus said. Thaddeus made a long pause, and Lucy interrupted, saying, "That's all?" Andy told her sister to be patient, and looking at Lucy, the little man said, "Don't trouble yourself, my lady; the best part is yet to come."

"Sorry, Thaddeus; please take your time," Lucy said. And Thaddeus continued.

"Later that night, King Noble and Queen Lydia were the first to arrive at the big hall to welcome their guests. Moments later, the trumpets announced the arrival of the Utopian Royalty, and everyone in the room turned their gaze towards the entrance, where King Percival, his sister Henrietta, and Prince Nolan were ready to enter the room. The three of them came wearing their masks. Henrietta had a hat with very long feathers that made her look like a peacock.

The announcer said with a deep voice, 'His Majesty King Percival, Her Royal Highnesses, the Grand Duchess Henrietta, and Prince Nolan from the Kingdom of Utopia.'

The crowd received the Utopian royals with prolonged applause, followed by a mixture of hurrahs and a few laughs because of Henrietta's ridiculous hat. Then, the expectation increased because Princess Morgana was about to enter the hall.

Nolan was particularly distracted, thinking about the beautiful girl he had seen at Crystal Lake, but his sense of duty was telling him he had to go through with this.

Then, the trumpets sounded again, announcing the presence of Her Royal Highness, Princess Morgana. Everybody in the hall directed their attention to the entrance to see her. Then the announcer said, "Her Royal Highness, Princess Morgana of Ambrosia, accompanied by Lady Lumi of the dwarf nation."

All the eyes in that room were on her, especially the Utopians. Nolan, who had not shown much interest until then, was impressed by the beautiful figure wearing a white dress and a white mask. His heart beat hard, and he didn't understand why. A few steps behind Princess Morgana, it was Lumi of the Dwarf nation, a petite lady in a green dress.

The princess crossed the room, heading for the main table, where the two royal families were waiting. As she passed, the guests applauded and whispered comments about her beauty. When she stopped before the table, her father, King Noble, removed his mask as a courtesy and presented his daughter to the Utopians.

'My good friend, King Percival of Utopia, Grand Duchess Henrietta, and Prince Nolan… allow me to introduce my daughter… Princess Morgana of Ambrosia!'

Returning the same courtesy, King Percival removed his mask, followed by his sister and Prince Nolan; when Princess Morgana removed her mask, Prince Nolan, in complete astonishment, dropped his mask.

He quickly bent down to pick up his mask, and while he was getting up, he saw the Princess and couldn't believe his eyes. King Percival, impressed by the beauty of his future daughter-in-law, said, 'You are as beautiful as you are charming, my child. Your Majesty, your daughter has become a beautiful and delicate flower only comparable with the beauty of this land!'

Then, utterly in disbelief, Prince Nolan approached Morgana and said, 'It is you! The lady at the lake!'

She looked at him and, almost mumbling, said,

'I-I… can't believe it…It's you!! I've been wondering all this time who you were.' Morgana responded.

Both royal families were confused; they didn't understand what was happening. For a moment, the two youths looked at each other so tenderly that everybody around them felt like they were missing something. Then Nolan took Morgana's hand, and they both said, 'It is a pleasure to meet you!'

******

Lucy interrupted, saying, "Ohhh… how romantic!"

Andy and the dwarves laughed after Lucy's remark, and Andy said, "Girls always have to say something."

"Don't worry, master, I understand," Thaddeus replied and then continued,

"The music began, and the young couple walked to the dance floor, took each other's hands, and began dancing. The two kings were watching them in total surprise because they were sure they disliked each other.

King Noble invited Henrietta to dance, and Percival did the same with Queen Lydia. Many of their guests followed them. In the center, the young couple was dancing, staring at each other tenderly, as if nobody else existed around them.

The rest of that night was like a dream for the bride and groom-to-be. They looked very much in love, but their parents were still confused since they believed they hadn't seen each other for almost ten years. This sudden and unexpected change would mean not forcing their children to get married. After a few dances, Nolan and Morgana returned to the royal table, and King Noble was the first to ask, 'I think an explanation is in order. What's happening between the two of you?'

Morgana turned to her father and said, 'Father, this is a miracle. You won't believe what is happening to us.'

'Try me, my dear daughter!'

Morgana told them what happened in the lake, and Nolan added some details, but their families couldn't believe it. When Morgana finished, both kings stood up and embraced each other. King Noble said, 'The prophecy is true; the two kingdoms will be unified by love. Look at these two kids!'

'You're right, Noble. We'll have a wonderful wedding this Saturday. Let us toast to that.'

King Noble signaled for the music to stop and proposed a toast. When everybody raised their cups, a roaring thunder reverberated through the area, followed by a strong wind through the windows. The wind blew out a few candles, interrupting the toast. Fear and confusion invaded the room. There was such a profound silence that we could even hear everyone's breathing. Suddenly, a crow flew inside the hall, cawing loudly, and left.

Immediately, it began to rain, giving the impression that the sound and strong wind were caused by the weather. Henrietta felt something else was happening, and she looked a little concerned.

After the commotion, everybody regained their composure. Then, they followed the two kings in the royal toast. Dinner was served, and for a moment, everyone seemed to forget what had just happened, except for Henrietta, who was so disturbed that she tried to share her feelings with her brother.

'Percival, my dear brother, something is making me feel uneasy. We should check if everything is secure at the Forbidden Mountain.'

When King Noble heard that, he intervened, 'My dear Duchess, I can assure you it's nothing to worry about. We took many precautions to prevent access to the mountain. Our soldiers will die before letting anybody pass! So, please don't trouble yourself anymore!'

'King Noble is right, my dear sister. Months ago, we decided to double the security for the mountain, so please don't worry about that, and be more cheerful. We have too much to celebrate,' Percival finally said, and Henrietta felt a little relief.

That night after the ball, Morgana was talking with Lumi and Alina. The princess couldn't believe the turn of events of that night; she felt happy and was very much in love with Nolan. Then, Lumi told her,

'This has to be your destiny, Morgana. Neither of you knew about the other. Now you two are so much in love!'

'You can't imagine how wonderful it is to have this feeling. It seems like I've loved him my whole life,' Morgana said.

'Oh, my Princess, we're so happy for you.' Alina replied.

In Nolan's room, the prince was talking to Basile and couldn't hide his emotions.

'My loyal friend, can you believe this? Morgana is the lady of the lake! It seemed like I had dreamed the whole thing. I was about to surrender to this marriage without knowing that Princess Morgana was the one who conquered my heart.'

'I told you to be more positive. Remember? I knew that something good was behind all this and that you'd be happy in the end… good for you, Master!'

Nolan and Basile continued talking for a long time until they finally fell asleep…

Chapter Seven: Zoltar's Return

That was the last peaceful night in Ethernia, and since then, we have had almost three hundred years of terror and darkness. Everyone was happy that night, thinking about the wedding, the prophecy fulfilled, and the evil lord would never return, but that happiness and peace were about to end. Zoltar was fully awake from his five hundred years sleeping in prison and had regained his full power. He was ready to destroy everything good in the land.

The following day, King Noble ordered a royal picnic in the castle's gardens as part of the festivities. The two royal families were there, accompanied by their guests. Around the city, the streets were fully decorated, and the atmosphere was joyful. People were ready to celebrate the biggest wedding in the history of the whole realm.

Meanwhile, Zoltar and Simon were finishing planning their next move, and both were getting ready to strike. He wanted to take everybody by surprise and appear when they were more distracted.

'My lord, now that you have your power back, when do we attack?' Simon asked.

'Tonight, my loyal servant. We'll attack tonight! We shall give them a surprise they'll never forget!'

'Very good, Master; we'll be ready… he-he-he.' Simon laughed diabolically."

******

Back in the attic, Andy began to show some disturbance. He felt like something was burning inside of him. Thaddeus noticed it, stopped the narration, and asked Andy, "Master, what's wrong? You don't look so good!"

"I have a strange feeling like something is about to happen. It's hard to describe."

"Master, you're the chosen one; you're supposed to save the land. That's why you are feeling what's about to happen. They're starting to get inside of you. From now on, you'll be more and more part of this story."

"Well, I'm already very involved, so let's get through it and start planning how I'm going to help these people," Andy said firmly.

"Well said, my Master. Let me continue now."

******

"The picnic was almost over when the last guest arrived. Lord Nikos, the dwarf chief, was accompanied by his wife, Liona, and their committee.

The two kings received the honorable guest, who greeted them very graciously. After the protocols, Nikos shared his concerns regarding the disturbances of the previous days. Both kings gave little importance to Nikos' concerns; they blamed the weather. Nikos wasn't too convinced about that and recommended caution. Then, he said to them,

'My wizard Simon has been gone for over a week; I no longer trust him. I found stuff in his cabin that proves he has been practicing black magic. I have the feeling he went to the mountains.'

'That's impossible, Nikos! We have doubled the garrison there; no human or dwarf could pass and still be alive!' King Noble answered.

'Ah, you just said it, Noble; no human or dwarf can pass, but what about any other creature?' Nikos questioned him.

'What do you mean, Nikos?' Percival countered.

'With black magic, he can transform himself into any creature and pass without being noticed by the soldiers.'

Both kings looked at each other. Percival responded, 'Don't trouble yourself, Nikos. We gave orders to stop anything alive from trying to get into the mountains; the soldiers know that very well.'

At that moment, a dark cloud covered the sky, and the wind blew strongly, forcing everybody to rush to the castle. On the way, Nikos yelled, 'I don't like this. We must be prepared!'

When Henrietta heard Nikos say that, she remembered what had happened the previous night and, without hesitation, went to her room. She needed to get something. Nobody knew she had been the keeper of a big secret for many years.

******

Twelve years before, on the day Queen Rose, the mother of Nolan, died, moments before her last breath, she called Henrietta to her bed. She asked everybody to leave the room, and when she was alone with her, she told her she had been a member of a secret order, and she was the last keeper of a ring, which in the right hands could save Ethernia if the Dark Wizard ever returned. Then Rose told her, 'I don't have too much time to explain; you'll have to trust me, Henrietta!'

'What's on your mind, Rose? But you're too weak -- you must rest!' Henrietta said.

'I know I'm dying, but you're the only one I trust. No one must know about this; promise me, based on your love for Nolan, that you'll never tell anyone about this. Please, promise me, Henrietta!'

'I promise, Rose. What do you want me to do?'

'You need to hide and protect this ring until the day the prophecy is fulfilled. If the Dark Wizard doesn't return by then, take this ring to Crystal Lake and throw it around the center. The good queen of the Lake should know what to do with it.'

Henrietta, wide-eyed, responded, 'So the legend is true; there are mermaids in the lake!'

'Don't repeat this, Henrietta; you have promised me. Keep the ring and protect it with your life if necessary. If Zoltar returns, you need to read the inscription inside the ring. That will tell you what to do, but only if he returns, understood?'

Henrietta couldn't believe what she was hearing. But without understanding the whole story, she took Rose's secret with her… and since that day, she hid that ring with absolute secrecy.

******

When Henrietta arrived at her room, she opened her trunk and searched for a small bag. The ring was there. By then, the wind was getting intense, and lightning flashed in the sky without a single drop of rain. All of the guests were already inside the castle.

The city of Ambrosia was soon covered in darkness, and everyone was confused. It was the middle of summer, and they had never had this kind of weather before in that season.

King Noble asked everyone in the castle to remain calm. The guests gathered in the big hall, and then, like the snap of two fingers, the storm stopped. In seconds, it was quiet. A sense of relief came over everyone in the castle and the city.

After grabbing the ring, Henrietta hung it on her necklace; she wanted to have it with her, just in case. She had kept her promise to Rose for all those years, and then she remembered what she had told her: *If Zoltar returns, read the inscription inside the ring and follow the message.*

Henrietta returned to the main hall, and when Percival saw her, he asked her, 'For God's sake, where have you been, Henrietta?!'

'I went to my chambers. I needed to get something; that's all, my dear brother!'

'I was worried about you, my dear sister. I saw you run and couldn't understand why.'

'Don't worry about it; everything is fine.' She finally said. But Nikos, standing between the two kings, wasn't convinced by this apparent calm. Something was bothering him.

At that time, Zoltar and Simon began to descend the mountain. The evil wizard wanted to test his power, and what better opportunity for him than against the garrison of soldiers who were celebrating, too? What happened in that camp was nothing less than horrifying; the soldiers didn't have any chance of defending themselves. Zoltar didn't show any mercy, and using his hands, he sent powerful spells, burning and destroying everything alive in the camp. Both garrisons were annihilated in a matter of minutes. After that, Simon told his master, 'Master, your powers are at full strength. We should go to Ambrosia now and take your revenge.' Once again, Simon laughed diabolically.

'Yes, Simon, you're right. Let's go and give them what they deserve for keeping me frozen for centuries in that mountain!' Zoltar cast a powerful spell, creating a black cloud. They jumped on it and began their journey to Ambrosia.

At the Ambrosia castle, everyone seemed more joyful except Nikos and Henrietta, who did not trust this apparent calmness. King Noble ordered drinks for everyone, and the music started playing again to release the tension and restore the happy mood.

Zoltar and Simon were traveling inside that black cloud faster than the wind. They were passing through the Emerald Forest at such speed that Ambrosia would be in sight in only a few minutes. Zoltar was so focused and determined that his eyes were practically on fire. He thought his yearned moment of vengeance was getting closer.

At the castle, and entirely against protocol, both royal families decided to lead their guests and started dancing. For a few moments, everything seemed so perfect, like it was meant to be.

By then, the Dark Wizard was passing over Crystal Lake, and the dwarves, whose village was closer, noticed a great disturbance in the air. They felt something was wrong and immediately tried to warn their Chief, Lord Nikos. Some dwarves can send messages to other dwarves using their minds, so one sent a message to Nikos, hoping their chief could sense it and warn the two kings about the imminent danger.

Then, Henrietta felt a vibration in her chest; the ring was trying to tell her something. She pulled her brother aside and told him, 'Percival, I'm feeling something terrible is about to happen. We have to protect Nolan and Morgana before it's too late!'

'What do you mean, Henrietta? The last thing we need is to create panic. Try to stay calm and enjoy the party.'

'You're wrong, my brother. Something bad is about to happen!'

At that time, Nikos and Liona had already received the message from their village, and they observed how disturbed Henrietta was. So, Liona came closer to her and whispered something completely unexpected.

'Your Highness, please come with us. He's coming, and you need to be prepared. Have the ring ready!'

'What did you say? I don't understand?' Henrietta almost yelled.

'We don't have much time. He should be here soon. Our people sent us a message that great danger is coming. Take the ring out and have it ready to read the inside when he appears!'

'Who's coming, and what do you know about the ring?' Henrietta firmly asked.

'Nikos and I are members of the Order of the Clover. We know you've been protecting the ring since Queen Rose died. We have to be sure that the ring and you are safe from Zoltar,' Liona said, looking very convincing.

Nolan and Morgana were dancing in the middle of the hall, enjoying the moment and talking about their future, when suddenly, King Noble made a sign ordering the music to stop. Then he made an announcement.

'Dear subjects and guests, King Percival and I have agreed to order a seven-day holiday in the whole realm to celebrate the royal wedding.' A big cheer by the crowd followed the king's words, and when Lord Pendleton asked for a big hurray for the young couple, a loud sound, almost like an explosion, interrupted the celebration and broke the castle's front door. Seconds later, a sinister laugh was heard, followed by a cold wind that blew into the hall, terrorizing everyone.

A black cloud drifted inside the hall, and everybody got gripped with fear. Henrietta took the ring out of her necklace. It was a golden ring with a black clover set on top.

The evil laugh was heard again, clearly coming out of the black cloud, striking everyone into panic. The cloud began to fade, and two figures appeared: one tall and the other much shorter. That was the confirmation of Nikos' fears. He told Henrietta, 'Read the inscription, now! These two figures are Zoltar and Simon!'

The inscription read, 'Two touches in the heart will protect you from harm.'

Henrietta put the ring on her right hand and approached her brother and nephew, and Liona followed her closely.

Zoltar finally appeared in his magnificent and terrorizing figure and started killing the soldiers who were trying to protect the royal families and their guests. He was throwing fireballs, making them fall dead instantly. Everybody in the room was so scared that they were petrified and did not make a move. King Noble was the first to confront Zoltar. 'Stop now! Your quarrel is with me. Let these innocent people go!'

'You aren't in a position to ask for anything, Noble! Now it's my time; the planets are almost aligned, and you haven't had your wedding yet, so there is no prophecy!'

King Percival immediately moved forward and replied, 'What do you want from us, Zoltar?'

'You two shall pay for what your ancestors did to me unless you submit total obedience to me and proclaim me the supreme ruler of this land!'

At that moment, Liona, who was behind Henrietta, asked her about the inscription on the ring. After she told her what she read, Liona said, 'We have to save Nolan and Morgana -- touch them with the ring twice on their hearts. It's our only chance to protect them!'

Noble and Percival looked at each other; they knew that submitting to Zoltar would mean the end of Ethernia. Therefore, they had to put up a fight, but how?

King Noble said in a defiant tone, 'Absolutely not! We'll never submit to you!' Zoltar looked at Noble, and his eyes turned red. Then, he yelled, 'How dare you defy me?'

To the astonishment of everyone there, two light volts darted out of his eyes, hitting Noble right in the heart. Percival grabbed the fatally wounded Noble and said, 'You'll pay for this, Zoltar.' The dark wizard also sent a mortal spell to King Percival.

Everybody looked in terror as their monarchs were lying on the floor in agony. Henrietta and Nolan approached King Percival, who, with his last breath, told his sister, 'I'm sorry… protect Nolan and Morgana. They're our last hope. Meanwhile, King Noble's last words to his family were, 'I love you… don't lose faith.'

Nolan reacted immediately by trying to attack Zoltar, but Henrietta stopped him, knowing he would die if he tried to fight the evil wizard. Then, she touched him twice in the heart before Nolan pushed her aside and yelled something unpleasant to Zoltar, who immediately threw a fireball at the prince. However, Nolan dodged it, avoiding it by an inch. Then, Henrietta grabbed Morgana and touched her twice in the heart with the ring, too.

The furious Zoltar, who usually never missed a target, threw another fireball at Nolan. A shield produced by the ring's power protected him, and he only fell, standing up immediately.

Morgana took her father's sword and tried to attack Zoltar when Simon sent a spell to her, but the protection of the ring reflected the spell to Simon, throwing him back at least ten feet.

When Zoltar saw that, he stopped. He knew something was wrong; the spells didn't work on the prince and princess. Then, he remembered about a powerful ring that belonged to the order that had imprisoned him five hundred years before.

'Who has the ring? Who's wearing the ring of clovers?' He yelled with his eyes full of hate. Looking around, he found Queen Lydia crying by her husband's body and yelled, 'You?' Lydia looked at him, frozen in panic, and then Zoltar threw a powerful spell, killing her instantly.

Morgana screamed, 'No, please, my mother, no!' But her screams were in vain. Lydia was no longer breathing…then Zoltar looked at Henrietta, who yelled, 'Don't you dare.'

Zoltar noticed the ring on her finger and instantly threw her the same mortal spell as Lydia. But the ring protected Henrietta, deflecting the spell back to the evil wizard, forcing him to dodge it, and killing one of the guests behind him. He knew then that he couldn't kill the bearer of the ring, so he ordered Simon,

'Take her, Simon… she has the ring! She'll give it to me!'

Recovered from the impact, Simon grabbed Henrietta by her arm and brought her closer to Zoltar.

No one knew the ring couldn't be forced out of the bearer, so she would have to give it voluntarily…

At that moment, Nolan, still a little dizzy, came to console Morgana, who was crying by her parents' bodies. Then, the Dark Wizard told them in an assertive tone,

'You two are coming with me now. And the rest of you, prepare to pledge loyalty to me. Your kings are dead, but now I am the supreme ruler of this land! Tomorrow, I will come back, and you all will choose between serving me for life or death!'

Zoltar, Simon, Henrietta, and the two princes were immediately covered by the black cloud and disappeared, shocking the remaining people. The king and queen of Ambrosia, the king of Utopia, and many people were lying dead. The scene was frightening, looking at the survivors picked up the dead bodies.

Chapter Eight: The Music Box

Zoltar left the castle, leaving death and frustration, taking the remaining members of the two royal families as prisoners, the ones he couldn't kill. He was returning to the mountain to plan his actions with them.

The people at the castle were afraid and confused. They didn't know what to do next; then one of the nobles yelled, 'We must do something. We can't let Zoltar get away with this. Where's he taking our prince and princess? We have to save them!'

'This is the end; we don't have enough power to fight Zoltar. We have to pledge loyalty to him!' Another noble yelled.

'Never,' Lord Pendleton exclaimed. 'We have to fight! Pledging loyalty to him means losing everything we have. We should die fighting like our kings did!'

Lord Zuku, the head counselor to King Percival, replied, 'Nonsense, Lord Pendleton! It'll be futile to resist. It will be suicide, for sure. We must negotiate with him; it's the only way to survive.'

'I'll never bow to that evil creature!' Lord Pendleton replied in a firm tone.

Thus, they were divided into two groups; one led by Lord Pendleton, who wanted to fight, and the other by Lord Zuku, who wanted to live and was willing to pledge loyalty to Zoltar.

By then, Zoltar had arrived at the mountain with his prisoners, at the same place where he had been captive for many years and then converted into his compound. When he entered the main cavern, he threw them around the center and said, 'I need that ring, Henrietta. Give it to me, or I'll hurt your precious nephew!'

'No. You won't do that! You know you can't hurt him. If you want the ring, you'll have to kill me,' she said bravely.

'You know I can't kill you, but I'll cut off your finger!'

Zoltar was ready to cut off her finger, but he didn't know how powerful the ring could be to protect its bearer. When he was about to touch her, a force struck him, and he was shocked and pushed back.

When Simon saw that, he couldn't believe his eyes. 'Master, what happened? Why can't you hurt this woman?' he asked.

Zoltar yelled, 'Ahh…damn it! This ring is more powerful than I thought. I need my book quickly. Simon, bring me the damn book!'

Simon gave the book to his master. Zoltar opened it and went directly to Chapter XX, which described how to counter weapons against black magic, one of which was the ring of clovers. Zoltar read with such attention that the expression on his face changed from frustration to a smile of satisfaction.

'Aha! Simon, I got it. On this page, it states that I can't kill or harm anyone who bears this ring or those protected by it. But I can enchant them, turning them into whatever I want, as long as it does not cause them harm. So, all I have to do is find a way to eliminate them from this land permanently.

He made a cage appear in the middle of the cave and put the three inside it. Then he said to Simon, 'Watch them! I'll take care of them tomorrow. I want to prepare myself for my coronation.'

Zoltar had only one thing more significant than his power… his ego.

That night, Nolan, Morgana, and Henrietta tried to comfort each other, but the way they lost their loved ones was too much to bear. Henrietta, who was a little more composed, told the young couple,

'I know how you feel; this hurt me as much as you, but he can neither kill nor hurt us. We're going to have to trust our destinies and be prepared. Nolan and Morgana, I'm very sorry about your parents, but we have to believe that they died for a purpose. Now, it'll be up to us to save this land. This ring keeps us alive for a reason, but I wonder what else I can do with it.'

Nolan, obviously impacted by his father's death, said to Morgana, 'I don't care how long it takes, but I swear on my father's soul that we'll get our revenge… someday, Morgana, I promise you with all my heart, this evil wizard, will pay for this!'

'Shut up, you imbecile. By tomorrow, you won't have any chance…he-he-he.' Simon said in a sarcastic tone

'You traitor! Let's see what the dwarves will do to you; now they know who you're serving! Nolan said.

The Dwarf Wizard turned around and, still laughing, said sarcastically, "Yeah, let's see…." He went back to his chair in the cavern's corner to keep watching the prisoners.

Morgana spent most of that night sobbing until she fell asleep in Nolan's arms, and for a few hours, they had some peace.

The following day, Zoltar came to see the prisoners, and looking at Henrietta, he asked her one last time, 'Henrietta, this is your last chance. Give me the ring, and no harm will be done to you, the prince or the princess, as long as you pledge loyalty to me!'

'**Never!** You can do as you please, but I'll never give you this ring!'

'You fool! You will pay for this! You'll never see your nephew or this land again!' Zoltar replied, visibly upset. He ordered Simon, 'Bring Henrietta!'

Nolan tried to stop Simon, but Zoltar's spell immobilized him.

When Henrietta was in front of Zoltar, he looked into her eyes and said, 'You will no longer see the people you love! You will be condemned to live eternally in a cell like I was. Your appearance will be so repulsive that you will hate your ugliness! Nobody will believe who you are!'

Then a powerful light came out from Zoltar's hands, striking Henrietta's body, and in a matter of seconds, she was transformed into an ugly older woman with a horrible hump, deforming her body. Her face and hands looked so disgusting that Nolan and Morgana watched with horror, trying hard not to puke.

Then, Zoltar and Henrietta disappeared; he took her to the other side of the mountains, an area called Death Mountain, facing the desert, where she had been living ever since, accompanied only by rats, scorpions, and serpents.

When he returned, he approached Nolan and Morgana, who were still frightened by what he had done to Henrietta. Then Zoltar said,

'Now, you two! So, you were about to get married to destroy me! Well, I'll give you my wedding gift! He raised his hands and yelled, *APARETUS MUSICUS INSTANT!*'

A beautiful wooden music box appeared on top of a table, and then he added, 'You're going to be together for all eternity, and you will dance for me anytime I want!'

The young couple looked at each other, and a terrible feeling invaded them. Watching everything closely, Simon immediately asked his Master, 'Master, what is this box?'

'I still have this music box from my Master Wizard, The Great Julius. I'll use it to enchant these two, so they'll always be with me, no matter where I go.'

'Oh, Master, you're a genius! Nobody will ever know where these two are… they'll never be found.'

'Yes! Everybody will believe they're dead so that no one will threaten me ever… ha, ha, ha.' He laughed and ordered Simon, 'Open the box and watch the power of my magic.'

Zoltar made a quick move with his hands, and the cage disappeared. Nolan embraced Morgana, and they only had time to say to each other once last time, 'I love you.' Then Zoltar looked at them and said, *'TRANSFENDU… IMMEDIATUS!'*

They started transforming into two little porcelain figurines when Zoltar transferred them into the music box. What Zoltar didn't notice was that the power of the ring, combined with the power of their love for each other, acted immediately, creating a counter spell and carving a riddle on the top of the inside of the box. After that, he ordered Simon,

'Take that box, and let's go to Ambrosia. Our celebration has begun.' And the two wizards started to laugh harder and harder, while everything in the cave returned to the way it was before...

A triumphant Zoltar returned to the castle in Ambrosia, accompanied by his loyal servant, taking the music box with the enchanted princes, apparently for eternity. His ego was full of pride. He knew nobody could challenge him anymore; the planets were already aligned, making him more powerful than ever. He was ready to take control of the entire realm of Ethernia.

By then, the nobles who wanted to fight had already left the castle hours earlier with the loyal fraction of the Ambrosian army and the dwarves. They were going back to Utopia to regroup, hoping they would have a chance to strike against Zoltar and free the prisoners.

When Zoltar and Simon arrived in Ambrosia, the city appeared to be a ghost town. Everybody was inside their houses, and no one dared to come outside. Only a small committee led by Lord Zuku was outside the castle to receive him.

'Where is everybody? I was expecting a better welcome!' Zoltar said to Lord Zuku.

'People are scared, your grace. This committee represents the two kingdoms. We're ready to pledge loyalty to you, oh mighty Zoltar!'

'Where are the other nobles?' Zoltar asked, eager to know why so few were on that committee.

'They don't want to pledge loyalty to you, sir.'

Lord Zuku's answer upset Zoltar, who yelled, 'How dare they defy my power? They will pay with their lives!'

Full of anger, Zoltar glared at the committee members, but none dared to look into his eyes. Then, he went inside the castle and took possession of the royal suite as his own. He told Simon and Lord Zuku to order Ambrosia's citizens to gather in front of the castle for a proclamation. He warned them that whoever defied the order would be punished.

By then, the loyal forces commanded by Lord Pendleton, which had traveled almost the whole night, were getting into the Emerald Forest, and the dwarves were traveling with them. Nikos wanted to get to the village and protect his people from Zoltar's rage.

In Ambrosia, Zoltar was proclaiming himself the new ruler of Ethernia, with the title of supreme emperor, in front of a hopeless and speechless crowd. When he finished, he looked at the people and said to them, 'I will show you an example of my power. I want you to remember what could happen if you don't obey me.' Then, facing the castle and raising his hands, he cast a spell, transforming the royal castle's beautiful white shape into the darkest and lugubrious one.

The people of Ambrosia looked at his demonstration of power in disbelief. Many cried in silence, wondering what their future would be like. Zoltar ordered Zuku to be the first one to pledge loyalty to him. In front of the astonished people, he transformed Zuku into an ugly creature he named General Morton, an 8-foot-tall ogre with a horrific appearance.

Zoltar ordered Simon and Morton to come with him. They went to the main square, where Zoltar used a powerful spell to create an army of goblins and trolls. Then, he ordered Morton to lead them against Pendleton and the dwarves.

'Master, your wish is my will; I'll destroy all the traitors!' Morton answered, then yelled, 'Ahhhhhhh!' and joined the army of goblins and trolls and began chasing the remaining loyalists of both crowns.

The dwarves arrived at their village in the forest, and Nikos immediately summoned the council. He needed them to start the ritual immediately to protect their village. Pendleton and the remaining loyalists continued as fast as possible to Utopia to alert the people about the imminent danger. They couldn't imagine that Zoltar already had an army at least five times larger than theirs and was traveling three times faster.

Minutes later, Nikos met with the council members in the center of the village. They initiated an ancient dwarf ritual that rendered the village invisible to everyone except them, relocating it to a different area in the forest.

At Ambrosia, the scared population passed in front of the castle one by one, pledging loyalty to Zoltar, under threats of slavery and death if they didn't. By then, the music box was already inside Zoltar's room, guarded by two trolls. No one except the servant Alina saw Simon placing it there, and she was ordered not to touch it. Alina, a clever girl, immediately assumed that the box was valuable to Zoltar, and she wanted to share that information with the only ones she could trust… the dwarves.

Morton's army was advancing relentlessly and was getting closer to the Emerald Forest. At that time, the council and Nikos raised their hands and yelled the final words, *'DISSAPARETUS,'* the village disappeared for everyone except them.

Later that day, Morton and the dark army arrived, but the village wasn't there anymore. They looked all over the area, but they couldn't find anything. A frustrated Morton yelled, 'Let's go! We'll take care of those dwarves later.'

Just before dusk, Morton's army finally reached Pendleton and the Loyalists. They were almost at the end of the forest, ready to move into the Utopia valley. They gathered around and fought bravely, but the battle didn't last too long; the Loyalists didn't have a chance, and everyone was killed. The last survivor was Lord Pendleton, who was fighting with two goblins. When Morton saw him, he yelled, 'He's mine!' And the goblins moved away, leaving the last loyal lord face to face with Morton; Pendleton was tired, but he fought courageously, even cutting three fingers out of the ogre's left hand just before Morton grabbed and killed him with his own hands. Morton and the dark army yelled in celebration, and then they continued marching toward Utopia to wait for their Master.

******

That night, in the forest, Alina the servant was already looking for the Dwarf village. She wanted to reach Lord Nikos and tell him about the box in Zoltar's room. It was dark, and she could hardly see where she was. Suddenly, her horse whinnied, making her fall. Alina tried to stand up, but then she felt a point of a lance, and a tiny voice asked her to identify herself. She knew that it was a dwarf patrol and looked in all directions, but she couldn't see anything; dwarves are masters in camouflage. Then, trembling, said, 'Please don't kill me. I'm a friend.'

The voice asked her, 'What do you want in the forest?' She responded, 'My name is Alina, the first maid of Princess Morgana, and I have important news for Lord Nikos. Please take me to him!'

'How do we know who you are?' One of the dwarves asked.

'I have the royal seal!' She said, showing the one she had taken from the king's room right before Zoltar came that morning.

Using a secret passage to the new location, the dwarves took Alina to their village. When they arrived, Lumi was the first to recognize Alina and immediately ran to her. The loyal servant told her, 'Lumi, I need to see your father. It is important.'

When they reached Nikos' cottage, he was reunited with his council; her timing couldn't have been better. Alina told them about the mysterious box in Zoltar's room, which seemed valuable to him. Then, she mentioned how the people of Ambrosia had been forced to pledge loyalty to the evil wizard. Nikos and his council were listening attentively, and when she finished, they all agreed that the box ought to be valuable and that they should find out why.

Nikos suggested that Alina return to the castle to avoid any suspicion from Zoltar. He told her, 'We need to find out why that box is so valuable. Also, we must find out what happened with Henrietta, Nolan, and Morgana.'

'Yes, Lord Nikos, I'll do my best to find that information…!' Alina responded.

'You'll have to observe him closely; any information you may get will be good. Now go before they notice that you aren't there. We'll take you to our secret passage; you will get there sooner,' Nikos said. Then he gave her a medal and added, 'Face this medal against the sun, and I'll know you have a message for me.'

Two dwarves escorted Alina through the secret passage to the city of Ambrosia and then helped her enter the castle without being noticed.

The next day, early in the morning, when Zoltar left the castle, heading for Utopia, Alina went immediately to his room. She wanted to check the box, but when she was about to open it, she heard footsteps approaching and quickly hid under the bed. It was Simon who entered the room to gather some items needed by his Master. When Simon saw that beautiful box, he couldn't resist the temptation and opened it. Then, looking at the two little figurines, he said, 'How do you like it now? Nolan and Morgana, you idiots will dance for us anytime we want.' Then he started to laugh.

He wound up the music box a little, and the couple began to dance. When they finished, he closed the box and left.

Alina was holding her breath, trying not to cry. She knew that if Simon had seen her, it would be her death for sure. Then she thought, *that's what happened to my Princess and Prince Nolan… Zoltar enchanted them in that box…! What a horrible thing to do… I have to tell this to Lord Nikos!*

She waited a few seconds and quickly opened the music box; she almost cried when she saw the two figurines. Taking a deep breath, she closed the box again and ran out of Zoltar's room. Without a moment to lose, she went to the closest window and quickly pointed the medal Nikos gave her against the sun, sending the signal to the dwarf lord.

******

Later that day, Zoltar arrived at Utopia. His army was waiting there, and no one resisted because they were too scared. After all the citizens gathered in the main square, he told them about the changes in the kingdom. Zoltar proclaimed himself the new supreme emperor and named Morton his deputy. By then, the people of Utopia knew the terrible fate that had befallen their beloved royal family, so, without hope, they pledged their loyalty to Zoltar.

That night, when Alina was working alone in the kitchen, she felt someone pulling on her dress twice. She turned around, but she couldn't see anyone. Then a tiny voice whispered, 'Alina, don't make any noise. I'm the messenger from Nikos. Let's go outside. No one should see you talking to me,' the dwarf was wearing a special cloak, making it difficult to see him.

Alina took a bucket and went outside to get some water. The dwarf followed her. When she stopped at the wheel, she quickly gave the little man a piece of paper, saying, 'Give this to Lord Nikos; it's important.' The dwarf took the paper and left immediately.

The messenger returned to the dwarf village as fast as possible. Upon arrival, he went directly to see Nikos and gave him the piece of paper. The dwarf chief unfolded it and began reading it aloud. The expression on his face changed when he finished, and his daughter, Lumi, seated by his side, began to cry. Nikos wrinkled the paper and said, 'We must get that box at all costs! We would bring it to safety and find a way to free the prince and princess. I'm going to see Fedora, the good queen of the lake, and ask her for advice; she's the only one who can tell me what to do next'…

Chapter Nine: The Secret Mission

The following morning, Nikos left the village, and headed for Crystal Lake. He went to see Fedora, the Queen of the Lake. A small group of dwarves were in charge of protecting him. Fedora was the only one who could help him; her magic was as powerful as Zoltar's, but only in the lake and the immediate surrounding areas, weakening as it moved away.

To reach Fedora, Nikos had to take a boat, usually hidden in a secret place by the lake, and row to a little island that moved around the lake. He would have to go alone; he knew Fedora didn't like to be seen or disturbed unless it was for something important.

When Nikos arrived at the secret place by the lakeside, the dwarves helped him to uncover the boat. Then he said to his escort, 'From here, I have to continue alone. I don't know how long it'll take me, so wait for me here.'

Nikos got in the boat and started rowing across the lake. He didn't know where he was going. About half an hour later, he encountered a cloud of fog that enveloped him, and moments later, he arrived at the small island, although it seemed like the island had found him. He stepped out of the boat and, using a magic shell, sent a signal to the mermaids. Then, he seated himself at the foot of the only tree on that tiny island; it was small but big enough to provide some shade. He waited there for one of the mermaids to come to him. Moments later, Fedora's daughter appeared, saying,

'Hello Nikos, it's so good to see you; it has been a long time since our last meeting. What can we do for you?'

'Thank you, Marily, it's good to see you too. I need to see your mother. I hope she doesn't get upset because she has to come to the surface. I know how much that disturbs her, but she's the only one who can help us save Ethernia from the evil Zoltar.'

'It's not a problem, Nikos. I'm sure she'll come as soon as I give her your message.'

Nikos waited for several hours, and right before sunset, when he was about to fall asleep, a reflection appeared in the water, catching his attention. The reflection started getting brighter and brighter. Nikos stood up and got closer to see it. He was sure Fedora was about to appear.

Then, a beautiful chariot made of shells emerged from the waters. Two giant seahorses pulled it, bringing out the magnificent Queen Fedora, the good witch of the lake.

'By the beard of Neptune, Nikos…! It's so good to see you again, my old friend.'

'Oh, Fedora, it's good to see you too. I've so much to tell you.'

'Tell me, my friend, I want to know; there is a great disturbance in my oracle. What is happening?'

'My dear queen, I have sad news to give you. The evil wizard Zoltar escaped days before the planets aligned and killed Noble, Percival, and Queen Lydia!'

'Zoltar escaped? I knew it. Only something like that could cause that kind of disturbance in the Oracle. This is terrible news.'

'Not only that, Fedora, he has also enchanted Prince Nolan and Princess Morgana and transformed them into porcelain figurines inside a music box. We don't know what he did to Henrietta, who had the ring of clovers."

'Damn it! We have a big problem now. I'm sorry about Noble and Percival – they were great Kings. Poor Lydia, too. I saw her once when she was a child!'

Nikos gave Fedora full details of all the tragic events. She listened carefully, and when he finished, she told him,

'First, we need to get that music box at all costs. I will consult the oracle to see what the future may bring and what to do with that box. Come to see me on the next full moon, and I'll tell you what to do next. In the meantime, let me give you this magical silver dust.'

A small box appeared, and Fedora gave it to Nikos. Then she continued, 'It's invisibility dust. A few grains on the head will do the trick, but it only lasts about two hours each time. Use it at your discretion.'

'Thank you very much, Fedora; this dust will help us to accomplish our mission. I also want to thank you for taking the time to see me. I knew you'd tell me what to do. I'll organize a group to get that box and bring it personally the next time I come to see you.'

Fedora returned to her chariot, said goodbye, and submerged into the water. Nikos got into the boat and was magically taken to the secret place by the lakeside, where his men were waiting for him.

That night, when they arrived at the dwarf village, Nikos called for a meeting with his council to discuss how they would steal the music box from Zoltar's room. It would be a dangerous mission, so he suggested that his two most trusted men…``

******

Thaddeus stopped for a moment. Then, looking at Andy and Lucy, he asked them, "Can you imagine who…?" After a pause, he added, "Luscious and I!"

"You guys? How old are you?" Lucy asked eagerly.

"Very old, Lady Lucy… very old!"

"How old?" Andy inquired.

"A few hundred years old, my Master… Now let me get back to the story."

Thaddeus continued as the siblings looked at him in disbelief.

"Thus, the council agreed with Nikos to give us that mission. But, of course, we'd need Alina's help.

We waited for almost two weeks, and we got a little impatient. Finally, one afternoon, Alina sent the signal, and we got the order to go to Ambrosia City and steal Zoltar's Music Box. We had to leave after dark since the secret passage would take us outside the city, and people could see us. Nikos gave us enough invisible dust for the two of us and the box.

That night, when we reached the back of the castle, we hid and waited for Alina to come out to the wheel to pick up water… She used to do that every night.

Minutes later, Alina came to collect water from the wheel, so we approached her with extreme caution. When she was filling the bucket, we called her, 'Pssst Alina… Alina… Nikos sent us; we need your help to get into Zoltar's chambers. Don't turn around now. We're invisible…'

Startled, Alina dropped the bucket, prompting one of the servants to ask her, 'What's happening? Are you okay?'

'Yes, I'm fine. I dropped the bucket. That's all!'

Then, she turned back and whispered, 'I've been expecting you for days. We have to wait until later tonight. Usually, I bring him a cup of tea every night just before he goes to sleep. He likes to play the music box for a few minutes, then puts it back in a chest and goes to the main tower to see the whole kingdom. It reminds him of all his dominions. When he returns to his chambers, he locks the chest and goes to bed. Outside his door are two trolls guarding it the whole night, so you must do it when he goes to the tower. With any luck, he won't open the chest again until tomorrow. So, you'll have about ten to fifteen minutes to get there and steal the box.'

'We'll wait for your signal.' I said, and pointing at the backyard window of the castle, I added, 'Wave your right hand by that window. We'll know it's time.'

Alina gave us the signal around midnight, and since we were visible again, we immediately put on a little more silver dust and ran into the castle. She was waiting in the back entrance, and when I whispered, 'Where?' She pointed us in the right direction and said, 'Follow me.'

As she told us before, we found two trolls guarding the door. Even though they couldn't see us, trolls have a great sense of smell, but since they are so dumb, they looked in our direction, believing no one was there. Inside the room, we went directly to open the black chest. Like Alina said, it was unlocked. We opened it with extreme caution, and without hesitation, we grabbed the music box. Taking a bag of dust, we dropped some on the box to make it invisible. Then, we left the room. Alina distracted the trolls, who smelled us again and acted a little uneasy, looking around and asking each other if something was happening. Since they couldn't see anything unusual, they returned to guarding the door.

On our way out of the castle, we passed some trolls and goblins without a problem. The trolls are too dumb, and the goblins don't have a sense of smell. When we were outside, we saw somebody coming in our direction, someone who could easily detect us and feel our presence. That was Simon… the dwarf wizard. We tried to avoid him, passing as far away as we could from him, but he suspiciously looked in our direction.

He didn't come any closer because he was hurrying to see Zoltar. When Simon got to his master's room, he told his master what he felt. Zoltar immediately jumped up from his bed and opened the chest. To his astonishment, it was empty.

'**Noooooooooooo!** The box! Somebody stole the music box!' He yelled and immediately cast a spell on the two guards, turning them into dust. Then, he ordered a search. All the guards were alerted, and the servants were ordered to report to the Castle's main hall. At that time, we were crossing the city, still invisible, and ready to take an old sewer tunnel to the river that goes to the forest.

By the time we reached the sewer, the invisible effects were almost over, but we could still enter the tunnel without being noticed. Moments later, we finally came out on the other side. The river was only yards away, and a boat awaited us. We jumped on it, and we went back to the forest.

In the castle, everybody was interrogated. Zoltar knew some persuasive methods to make people talk, but nobody told him what he wanted to hear. Finally, it was Alina's turn. He perceived that she was hiding something, but he couldn't get a word from her.

By then, we were entering the secret passage to our village. We were finally safe, and our mission was accomplished. It was almost morning when we finally arrived at our Village. Everybody was waiting for us: Nikos, the council, and all the dwarf people. When they saw us, it was like a hero's welcome. Our names were chanted, and hurrahs were heard from all over the village. Nikos received us with these words: 'Mission accomplished, my brothers… Welcome home!'

Chapter **Ten: The New Prophecy**

After a little celebration, we went back to reality. Our first thoughts were for Alina. We knew that as soon as Zoltar noticed the box was missing, he would start a massive search, and the castle's servants would be in trouble, especially Alina, who was in charge of his stuff. We were very concerned for her…-

Nikos called for another council meeting, and his first words were: 'We have in our possession the box containing our enchanted prince and princess. Our next task is to find out what happened with Duchess Henrietta and if Alina, the loyal servant, is still safe. We know that Zoltar couldn't kill Henrietta, but he could enchant or hide her… We need to know her whereabouts and what happened with the ring of clovers.'

One thing we knew for sure was that she didn't give it to Zoltar. Otherwise, he would have known how to find our village and would have destroyed us by then.

Later that afternoon, news arrived from the city. We had established clandestine communication with some loyal contacts in the city. They had been risking their lives, using the sewers to escape the city and meet with our messengers. The message said that Zoltar was very upset and had been punishing many servants in the castle. He believed the dwarves were involved in the disappearance of his music box.

When Nikos received the news, he ordered the immediate relocation of the village, and from then on, we've been relocating it almost every month to prevent Zoltar from finding us.

That night, Nikos called for two of the best young warriors, Valerix (Vale for everyone) and Kaleb, and ordered them to go to the city and find out what had happened to Alina. Nikos gave them some silver dust (invisibility dust) so they could use it to enter the castle.

When they arrived at Ambrosia, they put on the silver dust to become invisible. As they crossed the city on their way to the castle, they saw fear and sadness on everyone's faces. Most of the houses were dark, and nobody dared to have any lights on. It seemed as though the city of Ambrosia was a ghost town.

Using the back entrance to the castle, they went directly to the kitchen and waited until the servants came to eat. Fortunately for them, only a few minutes later, they heard the old cook tell the other servants, as they were coming into the kitchen,

'Poor Alina, this devil has transformed her into a black cat! Someday, he'll pay for all this!'

'Shhhhhh. Woman, don't say a word. The walls are heard in this castle; you could be the next! You better keep your thoughts to yourself and don't say anything,' another servant told the old woman.

'I don't care. I'm old, and I've already lived long enough. I'm not afraid of that monster! That evil midget Simon took her, who knows where?' the woman responded, very upset.

Vale whispered to Kaleb, 'Did you hear that? Let's go to the village; Nikos needs to know this.' Thus, they left the castle without delay. By then, the effects of the silver dust were about to wear off, so they needed to be in the sewers before they became visible again.

When they arrived at the village the following day, they went directly to see Nikos. Vale gave him the news; Nikos responded, 'I have to meet Fedora by the next full moon… that's only in a few days. We'll take care of Simon when I return from the Lake. He knows for sure where Henrietta and Alina are. You both did a good job!'

'Thank you, my Lord,' both dwarves said simultaneously.

In the following days, the news got worse. In the cities of Ambrosia and Utopia, people were punished simply for giving a bad look to the trolls. Zoltar was sending people to the dungeons for no particular reason. Everyone was living in fear and terror.

Thus, Nikos started to prepare for his next trip to the lake, planning the route and how they would hide the music box. Zoltar had been sending patrols all over the realm, searching for it.

******

Finally, the first day of the next full moon arrived. Nikos and his escort departed right after sunset. They wanted to travel in the darkness, so they planned to travel at night and through the darkest part of the forest. They traveled the whole night, taking short stops to rest. On their path, they came across two patrols, but helped by the silver dust, they managed to avoid them.

It was already midafternoon when they arrived at the spot by the lake where the boat was hidden. Nikos jumped on it, taking the music box, and without delay, started rowing, looking for the moving island. After almost half an hour of rowing, he landed on the tiny island. He took the box out, placed it by the only tree, and sat beside it to wait for Fedora to come out. Of course, he sent her the signal first, and she made him wait for almost an entire hour, which seemed endless; finally, moments before sunset, he saw the massive splash in the water, and the shell chariot came out, bringing Fedora from the bottom of the lake.

'Hello Nikos, my old friend, it's nice to see you again… I see you brought that music box, like you promised!'

'Nice to see you too, Fedora. I brought it, but I have something to tell you.'

Nikos told her about everything that had happened since their last meeting and how the people of the land were suffering Zoltar's cruelty. This news made Fedora sad, so she asked him to open the music box.

The dwarf lord opened the beautifully carved box, and Fedora's face changed when she saw those two porcelain dolls, perfectly identical to the prince and princess. She reacted, saying,

'Look at this poor couple…so young and in love, and now part of this music box, who knows for how long? Zoltar was so afraid of them that he wanted to have them as close as possible to him, so he enchanted them in this box. What he doesn't know is… that love always finds a way, and having them together will make their love even stronger. He is so evil that he underestimated the power of love!'

"We need to find a way to help them, Fedora… There must be something we can do!' Nikos responded

And Fedora continued, 'I've consulted the oracle, and nothing can be done now. We need to wait for the one marked by the clover. This box must contain some notes or clues to provide us with more information. I'm sure that when Zoltar did the spell, the protection of the ring must have put some counter spell somewhere in this box!'

Nikos looked inside the box and saw a tiny inscription on top of the little mirror at the center of the lid. He immediately told Fedora, 'Look over the mirror. I can see some inscriptions there, but the letters are too small.'

With a snap of her fingers, Fedora made a magnifying glass appear and read exactly what we had just read before I started telling you the story.

FULL MOON WILL HAVE TO BE, TO USE THE GOLDEN KEY… LET THE MOONLIGHT TOUCH THE BOX AND READ TWICE THE MAGIC WORDS. THE GOLDEN GATE WILL COME… AND YOU WILL ENTER OUR LAND TO FACE YOUR DESTINY…

'What does that mean?' Nikos asked.

'The oracle also told me that many moons and rains will come and go till the one marked by the clover will come to free the land, and that we have to let the box find its way!'

'I still can't understand, Fedora. How long will we have to wait, and who is this one marked by clover?' Nikos asked.

In her infinite wisdom, Fedora responded, 'It means that someday in the future… I don't know exactly when… a chosen one, someone marked by the clover, will come to break the spell and free Ethernia. He'll have to use a golden key, but I don't see any key here… so I can't understand that part!'

Suddenly, a light coming from the full moon reflected directly over the music box, and Fedora opened her eyes and, seemingly possessed, yelled, 'Aurus-Kiele!'

Then, pointing at the music box, she added, 'This key is for the one marked by the clover, who by his sixteenth birthday will become its master.'

A little golden key floated in the air on top of the music box, and a lock appeared in the front of the box. Still in a trance, Fedora took the key and said, 'Protectus Kiele proteus.' Then, a small black box appeared in her other hand, and immediately afterward, the light from the moon disappeared, and she woke up from the trance.

When she saw the key in one hand and the box in the other, she asked Nikos what those things were doing in her hands. Nikos repeated what she had just said and told her about the apparition of those things. Still confused, Fedora placed the key inside the little black box. Then, she said to Nikos,

'We have to protect these things from Zoltar! Most importantly, we can't allow him to have both. It'll be their destruction for sure. We have to separate them now. The people of Ethernia will have to wait and suffer! Unfortunately, generations will have to pass; there isn't another way; they'll have to learn to live like this for a long time. I'll set up a spell to limit Zoltar's power in the forest as much as possible! We have to wait for the chosen one… that's it.'

Then Nikos had an idea to place the music box as far away from Ethernia as possible, so he suggested entrusting the music box to the Leprechauns, and Fedora would take care of the key until the arrival of the chosen one. Fedora took a couple of seconds to think about it, and then she told him, 'Good idea, Nikos, I'll take care of this little box; you will contact me when the time is coming, and then I'll give it back to you, to be given to the Keymaster, and then we'll check with the oracle what to do next!'

'Consider it done, Fedora. I'll personally give the music box to Robix, the Leprechaun King, with precise instructions to take care of it and wait for the proper time, when the box will chart its course to meet its Keymaster.'

After saying goodbye, Fedora walked to her chariot and submerged in the lake. When she disappeared in the waters, Nikos returned to the hidden place, taking with him the precious music box that someday would bring the one who would save the land.

When Nikos arrived at the village the following day, his first order was to send Vale to contact Robix, the Leprechaun King, and give him a personal message. To meet with Nikos during the next full moon, somewhere in the passage to Britannia (Passages usually last longer during the full moon), to deliver a valuable package that needed to be in custody by the leprechauns.

Right after that, he summoned the council again. The new purpose was to find the whereabouts of Henrietta and Alina. They all agreed that the only way would be to kidnap Simon, get the information, and release him, all on the same day. This operation would have to be conducted in a way that neither Simon nor Zoltar would suspect anything, for the protection of both Henrietta and Alina.

About a week later, Vale returned from the Leprechaun country, bringing King Robix's answer. The king had agreed to meet our chief on the next full moon, using the passage to Britannia. Luscious and I were summoned to Nikos' cabin, where we were tasked with kidnapping Simon.

From our informers, we knew that Simon used to leave the city every Wednesday to go deep into the forest, but nobody knew where and for what reason. He was always escorted by a group of trolls, but only up to a certain point. From there, he continued alone. So, we planned to intercept him after that point and try to get the information we needed.

The following Wednesday, when Simon went to the forest, we waited for him there. When he passed our hidden point, we started to follow him at a prudent distance. He knew the forest well, but so did we. He was moving without leaving a definitive path, going erratically. When we finally reached the point where he would usually continue alone, we used our silver dust to become invisible and followed him. We knew he could sense our presence, so for that reason, we kept a reasonable distance from him.

He stopped in front of heavy foliage that looked like a wall. We were a few yards behind and still invisible. Then he said a few words we couldn't understand, and the foliage opened like a gate, uncovering an enormous cavern. We followed him inside, but at a proper distance. To our surprise, we discovered he was raising two little dragons, and by then, almost extinct. We backed off immediately. Dragons have a strong sense of smell and could have sensed our presence. We went outside to wait for him; we didn't have much time for invisibility, so when he came out, we knocked him down from behind so he didn't see us and tied him to the closest tree. Seconds later, when he woke up, we threw some red dust (dust of truth, prepared by Nikos) on him, and we started the questioning.

The dust of truth is powerful, but it only lasts a few minutes, so without a moment to lose, we began asking him what had happened with Henrietta and Alina, and he started to sing like a canary. Without blinking, he told us their whereabouts and what Zoltar did that night to Henrietta. We didn't believe him initially, but the more he told us, the more it made sense. Henrietta was sent to the unexplored part of the forbidden mountains, known as the Dead Mountain, where nobody from Ethernia had ever been, except Zoltar and possibly Simon.

We didn't have time to ask him about the dragons because he was about to wake up from the effects of the red dust (which also makes you forget whatever happens under its effects). We couldn't let him see us, so we knocked him down again, untied him, and left the area quickly. We had to pass through the group of trolls waiting for him. Our knowledge of the forest, combined with the natural stupidity of these monsters, helped us navigate through without being noticed.

We returned to our village as fast as we could. Nikos was waiting for us, so we gave him the news as soon as we arrived. He was horrified when we told him about Henrietta and Alina. Then, he gasped and told us, 'Well, my friends, the fate of this land is already set; we'll have to wait for the Keymaster to save it. Zoltar was smart to transform Henrietta and Alina and take them to Death Mountain, knowing that we can't go there; it is dangerous for anyone from Ethernia, human or dwarf. All we have to do is take this box safely to the Leprechauns. Someday, it'll meet the one marked by the clover and save this land.'

The next day, Nikos sent a message to Fedora, notifying her about the upcoming meeting with Robix, the leprechaun king, and the whereabouts of Henrietta and the ring. Fedora is also powerless in the

Dead Mountain; thus, since then, our only hope has been the new prophecy."

******

At the Attic, Andy interrupted, saying, "You mean they've been waiting all this time for the Keymaster?" Thaddeus responded, "Yes, master, you are our only hope now."

Andy sighed and said, "Let's finish the story. I want to know what I can do for them."

"That's the attitude, master," Luscious added proudly.

******

Thaddeus continued,

"Three weeks later, just before the next full moon, Nikos left our village, heading for the passage to Britannia. As he did before, he went with a small escort. They were carrying a precious cargo. The future of the land depended on the success of that journey.

Nikos took enough silver dust to protect themselves and the box. Four days and nights passed before they finally arrived at the passage to Brittania's entrance. They mainly stayed hidden during the day and traveled during the night.

This passage was located on the north shore of the land, almost at the sea. When they arrived, a leprechaun guard was already waiting for them to guide them to the rendezvous point to meet his King. They followed him for about two hours in that endless tunnel until they finally stopped somewhere in the middle.

The leprechaun asked them to wait there for his king to come. Nikos ordered his escort to sit and rest, so they made a circle, putting the music box in the center.

About one hour later, when the dwarves were sleeping, they were awoken by the sound of trumpets. The Leprechaun king was arriving. He was seated on his carriage, pulled by a group of leprechauns. When he saw Nikos, he approached him, and after embracing each other, Nikos said, 'Robix, my old friend, what a pleasure to see you again; it has been a very long time. I'm here to ask you a great favor!'

'Nikos, my friend, it has been a long time. It's good to see you, too. What can the leprechauns do for their brothers, the dwarves?'

'It's a long story, Robix, but the most important part is that… Zoltar, the evil wizard, has taken control of Ethernia; he has killed the king and queen of Ambrosia and the king of Utopia, and has enchanted the heirs to the thrones, Nolan and Morgana. They were transformed into porcelain figures inside this music box. For the sake of our land, I have to ask you to guard and protect it until the day comes when it'll find its course.'

'My friend, consider it done. We'll take good care of this box until a sign tells us what to do next.'

'Thank you, my old friend. Our people are eternally grateful to you and to the leprechaun nation!' Nikos said.

Then Robix ordered his guards to put the box on his chariot. After that, he offered Nikos and the dwarves the famous Leprechaun beer, so they took a few drinks to celebrate their meeting and the future of the land. When they finished, the King and the Leader of the Dwarf nation embraced each other again, and after a short goodbye, both delegations returned to their respective lands.

Since that day, the key and the music box have remained hidden. Life in Ethernia became darker and miserable; the people lost all sense of happiness. The only thing that kept them alive all these years was the hope of the new prophecy's fulfillment.

One night, over one hundred years ago, something unexpected happened at the Leprechaun's Cavern. It was during a full moon, and a big shadow in the shape of a clover appeared at the entrance of their cave. Then, outside, many traces in the shape of clovers started to appear, making a path.

Suddenly, Robix remembered what Nikos told him: *Until the box finds its course.* 'This is the sign!' he exclaimed, ordering a servant to place the box inside a black chest and follow the path of clovers.

Robix personally led the task; they followed the path of clovers while the full moon gave them enough light to see it. The path ended at the entrance of an old house in the northern Scottish countryside. It was almost midnight, so everyone was sleeping in the house. The leprechauns took the black chest inside and found the main hall full of trunks and boxes, so they placed it among them so no one would notice it. Then, looking at the box, Robix said, 'Goodbye and good luck on your new journey. We'll be watching you.'

The house's residents were preparing to come to America the following day, so many trunks and boxes were at the entrance.

That was how this chest came to this land and ended up in this house! It was brought by your great-great-grandfather, along with his collections of antiques. He traveled with so many boxes and trunks that he didn't notice this chest. The chest was initially stored in the gallery's storage room. Years later, without anyone noticing, we brought it to the attic of this house. Since then, it has been here waiting for you." Thaddeus sighed, and then Andy said,

"But how did you know you would find the chosen one here?"

"The chest has a path, and we followed. We came here a few times before you were born. First, when your great-grandfather was born, your grandfather came into the world, and finally, when your father was born, thinking they were the chosen ones, we didn't find the clover marks, so we always returned to Ethernia. When Lucy was born, she was the first girl in this generation. We thought it might be her, but when we saw her mark, it was a rose. We knew that another child would come soon with the mark of the clover because the rose is the symbol of hope. Then, Fedora gave Nikos the small box with the golden key and a note she had written. He used a special messenger to deliver it to your Nanny the day you were born, and that night, the gatekeeper hid them in the rose garden," Thaddeus explained.

Lucy, excited by what she heard, was the first to say,

"What a story! So, romantic and sad at the same time. It is indeed incredible! We must do something to help these people, Andy; they need us!"

"You're right, Lucy." And looking at Thaddeus, he asked, "What do we have to do, Thaddeus?"

"All we know for now is that you have to wait for the next full moon to read those magic words and open the gate, so I'll go back and ask our chief, Nikos, what your first task will be. Then, more clues and challenges will come. You'll have to face them one at a time."

"In that case, let's put everything back in its place. We don't want anybody to see this; it'll raise too many questions we don't know how to answer." Andy said.

After fixing the attic as before, Andy and Lucy returned to their rooms. It was already way past midnight. One thing on their minds was what challenges may lie ahead for them.

Chapter Eleven: The Christmas Gift

The next morning, when Andy's parents woke up, they felt as though they had been sleeping for days. Helen and Conrad were still yawning when she said, "I haven't had such a good night's sleep in months. I feel great!"

"Me too, dear… Ohhhh, I slept like a log… Mmm, I can smell the fresh coffee that Helga is making. Let's go down and have some breakfast; I'm starving," Conrad replied.

Mrs. Muller was already waiting for them with the coffee ready, and like every Sunday, she had prepared her delicious biscuits.

Conrad said to her, "Helga! Good morning. Did you see the kids already?"

"No-no, sir, and it's almost ten thirty. I wonder what is happening. They went to bed early, and today is biscuits day, their favorite!" Helga replied.

"Yes, you're right, Helga. That's very unusual, but we also overslept," Helen said.

"You want me to check, sir? Why are they not awake?" Helga asked.

"Don't bother yourself, Helga. Give them a little time. They'll come soon; you know how they love your biscuits," a very relaxed Conrad said.

Andy was starting to wake up by then, and his two little friends were already at his bedside. Almost at once, they said, "Good morning, Master. Did you sleep well?"

"Never mind that… I thought about that box the whole night and what I had to do next. I fell asleep very late; it was almost dawn. I'm tired right now!"

"You better go downstairs now before they wonder why you haven't come to the kitchen yet on biscuit day!" Thaddeus replied.

"Oh my God, you're right, I better hurry up. Luscious, go and wake Lucy and tell her to come to the kitchen. Okay?"

"As you wish, Master," Luscious replied.

Andy grabbed his robe and went downstairs to join the rest of the family. Luscious went to Lucy's room and, moving her arm, said, "Wake up… wake up, Lady Lucy, it's time for breakfast! Master Andy and the rest of the family are already in the kitchen."

When Lucy opened her eyes and saw the little guy, she almost yelled. Luscious had to cover her mouth. Then she sighed and said, "Oh my God, you're real. For a moment, I thought that it was all a dream. What's going on?"

"Everyone is waiting for you in the kitchen, my lady; it's biscuit day."

"Yes! It's Sunday. Oh my God, biscuits day!" she yelled, jumping out of bed, grabbing her robe, and running to the kitchen. At the table, everybody was commenting about Andy's party. Andy and Lucy were looking at each other, thinking, *what if we tell them what happened last night... most certainly, they won't believe us.*

So, they enjoyed the rest of the breakfast, laughing and talking about their plans for the Christmas season, a huge tradition at the Logan home. Conrad and Helen are crazy about Christmas. They decorate their home beautifully yearly and throw a big Christmas Eve party for family and friends.

After breakfast, Andy asked Lucy to follow him. When they got to his room, he closed the door. Before he was about to say something, Luscious and Thaddeus appeared again unexpectedly before them, making Lucy and Andy almost jump out of the impression.

Then, Lucy told them, "Can you please stop appearing like this? You scare me to death!"

"Sorry, Lady Lucy, we don't have too much time. We have to go now; we'll return two days before the next full moon with your first task. Please take care of yourselves!"

"What about the box... Do I have to do something?" a very concerned Andy asked.

"You already have the golden key, Master. Take care of it; we'll open the gate on the next full moon. By then, we should know what to do next... bye, Master... bye, Lady Lucy."

"Bye, guys, see you soon!" Andy and Lucy chorused.

After the dwarves disappeared, Lucy returned to her room to get dressed. After lunch, she spent most of the afternoon talking to Andy about the fantastic story they had heard the night before. She inquired about the dwarves, asking Andy how long he had been in contact with them.

"Remember my seventh birthday when I told you about the two little guys in my room, and you told me I was too old for imaginary friends?"

"Yes, I remember it very clearly. You told me about them, and I didn't believe you... amazing! I understand why you always liked playing alone."

"Yes, until the day they disappeared on me. I was only eight years old, and I cried every night for months. Remember? Mom and Dad thought I was crazy, crying for my two imaginary friends that just left me."

"Mom and Dad were worried about you and decided to take you to a shrink," Lucy said.

"Those were hard days for me; kids laughed at me at school. The only good thing came when the McKenzies moved across the street, and I met Danny. Finally, after a while, I convinced myself that the dwarves were a product of my imagination! Then, all of a sudden, they reappeared this year on Halloween night."

The siblings spent a few hours in Andy's room, which surprised their parents. They couldn't recall the last time Lucy spent any time talking to her younger brother.

The following day, Andy met Danny at the bus stop. On their way to school, they talked about what happened Saturday night after Danny left. To avoid any strange looks, they sat in the back of the bus, and Andy continued the story, providing only a few details to avoid drawing the attention of the other students on the bus.

Danny was astonished and could hardly believe the whole thing. He asked Andy if he could spend the night of the next full moon, see this magical music box, and see what his first challenge would be. Andy responded, "Let me check with the guys, and I'll let you know." He, of course, was referring to Luscious and Thaddeus.

During the following weeks, Lucy spent most of her time preparing for her semester final exams at Harvard, so she almost forgot about the dwarves and the music box. She didn't have time to talk about it, spending most of it studying and revising her lessons.

Andy spent most of those weeks helping his dad and mom decorate the house (one of the best at Green Meadows). There wasn't a car that wouldn't stop to stare at the beautiful display of lights of this landmark in Concorde.

The first day of the next full moon would be two days after Christmas, so Andy had the time to help his parents without distractions.

******

Finally, Christmas Eve arrived, and Logan's Christmas party. That afternoon, Andy was getting out of the shower when suddenly, his two friends appeared dressed in green and red. They both knew the traditions in this world and told him at once, "Hello, Master, Merry Christmas!"

Just like before, the dwarves scared the crap out of Andy. Who told them, "Guys, one of these days you'll give me a heart attack!"

"Sorry, Master!" the dwarves replied

"Never mind that, let me get dressed now. I have to go downstairs to help with the party. The full moon starts in two days. Do you know what my first task will be?"

"Yes, master, but we'll tell you that later. Now, enjoy the festivities. Luscious will go to Ethernia to get final instructions from Nikos. Meanwhile, we'll start preparing everything for your journey. We'll see you after the party!"

"Okay, guys; see you later, and Merry Christmas!" Andy told them as he left the room.

At that time, Lucy was coming out of her room, too. Andy looked at her, motioned with his head, pointing at his room, and said, "Hey, Lucy, guess who already arrived?"

"Let me guess, the little guys?"

"Yes, and they scared me to death as usual. I'll see them again after the party."

"Okay, but let's go now. Our grandparents are here already, and Mom and Dad are waiting for us!"

So, they went downstairs and joined the party. Soon after, all their closest relatives and friends arrived, including the Mackenzies. Everybody was having a good time; the food was delicious, and they drank a lot of eggnog. Andy and Lucy got together with their parents and started giving candles to everyone, inviting them to go to the living room, where a beautiful ten-foot-tall Christmas tree stood beside the chimney, surrounded by presents.

Then, Helen invited everyone to gather around the piano, and they started singing Christmas carols. Cake and chocolate were served to everyone after that, and then they began to open the presents that each Secret Santa had brought to the party.

Andy and Lucy were having so much fun that, for a moment, they didn't think about the little guys and what they needed to do on the next full moon.

Finally, when the party was over, Lucy and Andy went to their rooms, carrying their presents. A big surprise was waiting for Andy when he opened the door… he found a mysterious present on top of his bed. The wrapping paper was unique, with different tones of green. It was a nice-sized box tied up with a red ribbon and golden glitter. It was so beautiful that it appeared as though the package was glowing. Andy left the presents he was carrying on the floor and immediately grabbed the package on his bed. It had a card on top that said:

"To the Keymaster, good luck in your first task!" At that precise moment, Thaddeus appeared in his room and said, "That present is from Lord Nikos, Master Andy!"

"Wow, I don't know what to say, Thaddeus; I've never seen such beautiful wrapping paper! Thank you very much! What's inside? I'm curious to know, but a little afraid to open it!"

"Don't worry, Master. Open it and see what's inside."

When Andy was about to unwrap the package, he touched the ribbon, and suddenly, it started to unwrap by itself, humming a beautiful melody. The package was enchanted. Andy let go of the gift and stepped back, his mouth agape in astonishment. The gift was unwrapped by itself; the paper was rolling back like new. Then, the ribbon started to make a nice bow around the roll.

In front of him was a nice wooden box about two and a half feet long, one foot wide, and no more than eight inches high. He hesitated, and when he was about to open it, Lucy knocked on his door, asking, "Andy, can I come in?"

"Come in, Lucy! I have something to show you!" Andy replied.

When Lucy saw Thaddeus seated on Andy's chair, she knew something was happening, so she asked her brother, "What is it, Andy? Let me see it."

"Look at this box on my bed. It was sent to me by the Dwarf Lord!"

"Wow, Andy, that box looks beautiful. Go ahead and open it to see what he sent you."

Andy started to breathe heavily and approached his bed. He opened the box and found a set of clothes, shoes, and a small leather case.

He had never seen these kinds of clothes before. When he pulled the garments out of the box, Lucy smiled and said, "Wow! What beautiful antique clothes. You'll look like a medieval knight."

"What is this, Thaddeus?" Andy almost yelled.

"Oh, Master, you'll need the proper clothes and shoes to go to Ethernia. You can't wear the pants and fancy shoes (sneakers) you wear every day."

"Don't tell me that I have to wear this. I'll look like a clown… and what's inside this leather case?"

"Don't trouble yourself, Master. You'll be dressed like any other lad from Ethernia and won't bring any attention upon yourself. But these aren't ordinary clothes. These pieces have been specially made for you. They'll protect you from any weather. The shoes can make you run faster than any other man, so you would get out of trouble if you encounter dangerous animals. Finally, in that leather case is the Dagger of Truth," Thaddeus said.

Andy opened the case and found a beautiful small silver dagger with a hilt shaped like a dragon's head and two emeralds set in the eyes. He was speechless. Then Lucy asked Andy to show her the dagger. When she saw it, her eyes glowed, and then she asked the dwarves, "Why do you call it the Dagger of Truth?"

"Because only the true chosen one can use it without missing the target." Luscious appeared at that moment, answering their question.

Still impressed by that beautiful dagger, Lucy told her brother, "Mom and Dad are about to come up, so you better put everything away. We'll talk tomorrow."

When Lucy left Andy's room, Luscious arrived and said, "I'm bringing a message from Nikos. He said that the oracle had spoken, and the best time to open the gate would be the first night of this full moon, precisely in two nights. Now we can give you information about your first task.

"Don't make me wait," Andy replied

And Thaddeus said, "Your first task is to free Henrietta and get the ring of clovers."

Andy remained silent for a few seconds and said, "Wow… that seems like a huge task. How in the world will I be able to do that?"

"Don't worry now, master, it will present itself. Besides, Nikos will help you too." Thaddeus answered, and after a long pause, Andy finally said, "I'll go to sleep now. I'm tired; I'll need all the rest I can get."

"Good night, master. Have a pleasant dream. See you the day after tomorrow!"

The next day, after they rested almost the whole morning, the Logans went to the Christmas Day party at the Mackenzies. Of course, Andy used the occasion to update Danny with the latest news, but most importantly, it would be time to open the gate in only twenty-four hours. Danny was thrilled about the whole thing, mainly because he would spend the next night at Andy's.

That night after the party, when Andy went to bed, he finally realized how difficult the task ahead would be and couldn't sleep. After almost an hour, his two little friends, who had been watching him, decided to help him a little. Using their flutes, they played a soft melody that only Andy could hear, putting him to sleep in no time.

Andy spent most of the next day with his two friends, preparing himself for the journey to Ethernia. He was so excited that, to calm him down, Thaddeus told him, "Master, don't worry. You won't be alone. We're going to be with you almost all the time!"

"What do you mean by almost? I thought you were going to be with me all the time…"

"There's an area in the Forbidden Mountains where dwarves can't go, so you'll have to go there alone!"

"Can Lucy or Danny come with me tonight?" he asked.

"No, Master, you're the one marked by the clover, so the only one who has to go and find Henrietta!"

"Well… in that case, I must be ready!" Andy responded in a concerned tone.

Later that afternoon, as expected, Danny came, bringing his stuff to spend the night. He was dying to see the music box, but most importantly, to know Andy's first task and hopefully meet the dwarves.

At dinnertime, when everybody was enjoying the dessert, something utterly unusual happened. First, the wind started blowing strongly, and then, a strange sound, like a whistle, was heard, followed by a female voice whispering: *KEYMASTER… THE TIME HAS COME… BE READY TO FULFILL YOUR DESTINY!*

Andy immediately looked at Lucy to see if she had heard that. She returned the look and winked, confirming his feelings. But, when he was about to ask the others if they had heard it, Lucy nodded, motioning for him not to say anything. What neither she nor Andy noticed was that Danny had also heard it. The poor guy was speechless and looked pale; the rest heard only the sound of the strong winds. So, Conrad told Andy, "Andy, please go and close the window in the hall before the wind comes in and breaks something!"

"Yes Dad... Hey, Danny, come with me," Andy said, looking for an opportunity to ask Danny if he had heard anything.

Andy and Danny left the table. On their way to the hall, they looked at each other and whispered, "Did you hear that?"

"That was creepy, man, I heard it very clearly!" Danny said.

"It sounded so real that I thought that Mrs. Muller and my mom would freak out and yell, but it seems like they didn't hear anything," Andy replied.

"When I heard it, it scared me to death, but then I saw your mom and dad act so natural, I knew they didn't hear it, so I decided to keep my mouth shut before they thought I was crazy," Danny said.

To their surprise, all the windows in the hall were closed. They looked at each other, and Danny was the first to say, "How come, dude?" And Andy told him, "Don't say anything. I don't want them to start asking questions; I'll ask the dwarves later."

Later that night, when Conrad left Andy's room after saying goodnight to the boys, Luscious came and told Andy, "Master, it's time; you have to get dressed. I'll take care of your parents and the old lady now. Thaddeus will come soon."

Andy pulled the box with the clothes sent by Nikos out of his closet, and just before he put it on, told Danny, "If you laugh, I promise you won't come anymore! Understand?"

"Okay, I won't laugh. I'm your best friend, right?"

When Andy began putting on the clothes, instead of laughing, Danny looked in disbelief and said, "Wow, man! You look great, like a swordsman from one of those action movies."

"Don't tease me, man. I look like a clown."

"That isn't true, dude," Danny said.

Andy was wearing dark tie pants, a white shirt with wide sleeves, reminiscent of a swashbuckler's shirt, a cape with a hood, a pair of short boots, and the Dagger of Truth.

"Well, we have to wait for Luscious and Thadeus to go to the attic," Andy told Danny.

Suddenly, they heard somebody knocking at the door. They opened it, and it was Lucy. When she saw her brother in those clothes, she hugged him and said, "You look very handsome, kid brother!"

"Thanks, Sis!" Andy responded. Then the dwarves appeared in the room, and Luscious reported that Everybody else was sleeping. So, Thaddeus added, "Let's go now… Master, don't forget the golden key."

"It's on my night table," Andy took the key from his drawer, and when they were about to leave the room, all of a sudden, Danny started seeing the dwarves and looked at them so stunned it seemed that his chin was about to fall all the way down to his knees. He couldn't talk on their way to the attic.

When they got to the attic, Danny finally recovered his voice, and they briefly laughed. There wasn't much time for that. The full moon was so bright that its light shone through the window, illuminating the center of the room, so they needed to move quickly. After pulling the black chest out and putting the only table in the attic in the middle of the room, they took the music box out and placed it on top.

Danny was watching the whole thing, completely speechless. He couldn't believe his own eyes. First, he was finally seeing the two dwarves, and second, the magnificent music box, spotlighted by everyone's flashlights.

Snapping out of the impression, he finally said, "Why don't we turn the lights on?"

"We need to let the moonlight illuminate the box. If we turn on the lights, they'll interfere," Andy answered, and then added.

"Before we open the box, I have a question for you, Thaddeus,"

"Yes, Master, what do you want to know?"

"What was that whisper we heard tonight, and why did only Lucy, Danny, and I hear it?"

"Master, that was a message from the mermaids, and the reason you could hear it is simple: you three believe in our story. The others don't know anything about it. Therefore, they don't believe in it. That's also why the three of you can see us, and they can't," Thaddeus explained.

"But they heard the wind," Andy replied, and Thaddeus answered, "The mermaids did that to distract them."

Andy turned towards the box and, taking the golden key, he opened it and said,

"We need the moonlight to illuminate the inscription. Let's move the table a little so the light can hit directly on the box; guys, give me a hand!"

Everybody helped him. Even Lucy pushed the table a little. Finally, when the light was facing the inside of the box, something unique began to happen. Green smoke swirled from the box and began to concentrate at the center of the room. Everyone watched in shock. Even the dwarves looked quite impressed.

They couldn't imagine what they were about to see… the green cloud was getting thicker and thicker and thicker!

Chapter Twelve: Aura Gate

Everyone in the attic looked at that green cloud with open mouths without making any noise. It was so quiet that the spiders could be heard walking around. Suddenly, the green cloud began spinning in circles, writing letters in the air. Lucy was the first to yell, "Hey, look! I think it's writing something."

"Those are the magic words, Master. You have to read them twice as soon as they're clear for you because they'll disappear soon after," Luscious told Andy.

When the words became clear, Andy read the following:

AURA GATE... AURA GATE!

Instantly, a green light came through the small window, illuminating the center of the room, and the floor started to rumble. The three youths panicked, especially Lucy. The dwarves tried to calm everybody down. When the rumbling stopped, the floor opened, and a door emerged in the center of the attic a few feet in front of the table.

It was an oval golden door engraved with symbols that no one in the room had ever seen. It was no taller than seven feet high and approximately four feet wide. It had a lock in the middle with a huge emerald right on top of it. The edges of the door were glowing so much that they couldn't see the rest of the room anymore.

Everyone looked at each other, but no one made a single move. The gate to another world was right in front, a world that only exists in our dreams or fantasy books, and where everything seems possible.

Thaddeus approached Andy and pulled his shirt to get his attention. He told him, "Master, go ahead, use the golden key to open the door!"

Andy nodded and said, "The same key?"

Thaddeus answered, "Yes, Master." Then, Andy started walking towards the door and took the key out of his pocket. Lucy and Danny were still frozen in wonder. When Andy finally inserted the key into the lock, to everyone's astonishment, the emerald came alive and opened like a mouth; it asked him in a female voice,

"ARE YOU ... THE KEYMESTER?"

"Yes, I am," Andy replied.

"GO AHEAD... OPEN THE DOOR!" the Emerald responded.

Andy unlocked the door and started to open it. All they could see was something like a multicolored portal. Then the Emerald said,

"WELCOME... MASTER!"

Andy looked at his sister and told her, "Bye, Lucy. Don't you worry, I'll be back."

Lucy immediately hugged his brother and said, "Good luck, Andy. I'll be waiting right here!"

Danny also hugged Andy and wished him good luck. Then, looking at the two dwarves, Andy told them, "Let's go, guys. Ethernia is waiting!"

"You're right, Master... to Ethernia!"

Luscious was the first to enter, disappearing as soon as he passed through the portal. Andy and Thaddeus followed. When Andy and Thaddeus disappeared, the door began to close, leaving our friends on their way to a magical world.

When the door closed, Lucy and Danny were astounded. What they had just seen was beyond their imaginations. Their brother and friend, respectively, had just crossed the portal to another world…They remained like this for a few seconds until Danny broke the silence, saying,

"That was awesome! Could you believe it, Lucy?"

And as he finished saying that, something unexpected happened. They heard a tiny voice telling them, "Hey, you giants…Could you tell us where we are? And what are we doing in this music box?"

Danny and Lucy turned around, and what they saw was as shocking as what they had just seen. The two little figurines were waving at them inside the dancing area of the music box. Lucy almost fainted, and Danny exclaimed, "Wow! Talking dolls! This is awesome!"

"They're not talking dolls, you dummy! They're the enchanted prince and princess! Something happened when that door opened, which made them come to life."

Then Lucy approached the box and said, "You've been enchanted by the evil wizard Zoltar. My brother has just entered your world to find a way to help you."

"Oh yes, I remember now. That terrible day in the cavern, he did something to us. I can't remember anything else after that," the little Nolan told Lucy.

Then Morgana whispered something to Nolan, who said, "You're right, my dear. Pardon my rudeness, giants; I forgot that introductions are first! May I present Princess Morgana of Ambrosia, and I am Prince Nolan of Utopia. It's a pleasure to make your acquaintance." Morgana and Nolan bowed at the same time.

"I'm Lucy Logan, and this is Danny McKenzie. We're both from Concord, Massachusetts, USA. It's also our pleasure to make your acquaintance… and we're not giants," Lucy said politely.

"It's a pleasure for me, too," said Danny.

"You're the ones that have been enchanted to that size, and that's why we look like giants to you," Lucy explained.

"Can you tell us more? Please…?" Morgana asked.

Then, Lucy began to tell them everything she knew about their sad story. She mentioned the new prophecy and that her brother, Andy, had been chosen to be the Keymaster of the gate to Ethernia because he was the only one who could break the spell and free their land.

******

On the other side of the portal, Andy and the two dwarves were coming down a long tunnel to the magical world of Ethernia. It was very dark and foggy, and they couldn't see each other, but they were talking and always felt each other's presence.

The smell inside that tunnel was like a fragrance of meadows and flowers. After a few minutes, they started to see a small light at the end, and Andy asked the dwarves, "Hey guys, I can see that light at the end. Does that mean we're getting closer?"

"Yes, Master, we have a few more minutes to get there. Now listen carefully... When we reach the end, the exit will open only for a few seconds, so we have to jump quickly. It's tricky because it looks like a high jump, but it's only three feet high. Don't look too much and jump... if you look too much and don't jump, the tunnel will throw you out anywhere it wants, and it could be painful. Do you understand?"

"How do you know that if you've never used this tunnel before?"

"Because this tunnel is similar to the others, we usually use it to get there. The difference is that the Golden Door was the only one that let you pass through it. You couldn't use the other portals."

"Okay. I get the point."

When they were finally approaching the end of the tunnel, the breeze started to get stronger. Then, the little hole began to open more and more, and they could see the forest, looking like a jungle with many dark and ugly trees, some in horrifying shapes and full of thorns. Thaddeus told Andy, "Master, that's the Emerald Forest! It used to be beautiful, but with all the plagues that Zoltar has sent over the years, it has become a horrible place. Only the area around Crystal Lake remains the same, thanks to the power of Fedora. Be ready to jump at any time now, Master."

"Wow... I've never seen anything like it before!" Andy stated.

"Get ready; we jump on three. Okay?" Luscious told them.

Suddenly, Andy felt fear strike him when he saw the exit; it looked like at least a twenty-foot drop, and he hesitated. Thaddeus grabbed his hand and yelled, "Don't look! Close your eyes and jump! One, two… three!"

Andy closed his eyes and jumped (it was Luscious who pushed him). Then, the three of them landed close to a huge tree surrounded by bushes full of spines. Andy opened his eyes and saw in amazement how the tunnel was disappearing behind them. It looked like the sun was starting to come out, and Andy, confused by that, asked, "Guys, we left about 15 minutes ago. Why is it already daylight?"

"Because we just crossed into a different dimension, Master. Time is different here," Thaddeus answered.

They began to walk through the dark part of the forest, surrounded by giant trees and enormous bushes. It was early morning, and a heavy fog covered the area. They were searching for the secret passage to the dwarf village, which was frequently moving, to avoid being found by patrols sent by Zoltar over the years to destroy the dwarves.

Thaddeus, who was a few meters ahead, found the entrance between two willow trees covered by bushes marked with a black mushroom. Then, he signaled Andy and Luscious to hurry up. When the three of them were in front of the gate, Thaddeus waved his right hand, and the black mushroom started to swing. Then he yelled, "*Ludibikus In!*"

The green wall of bushes opened, revealing the secret passage to the dwarf village.

They quickly entered the passage. Andy was only moments away from his first meeting with Lord Nikos and the rest of the dwarf nation. Soon, he will start to fulfill his fate in this land…

Chapter Thirteen: The Dwarf's Village

The secret passage was like a maze or labyrinth, about 4 feet wide, with the walls made out of tall bushes with plenty of thorns. Thaddeus was walking in front, guiding the group; Andy was behind him, and Luscious was at the end. Then, Thaddeus warned Andy:

"Master, don't touch the bushes; they're poisonous. Please walk in the middle of the path behind me!"

"Poisonous!? Thank Thaddeus, I'll be careful."

Andy looked a little nervous and anxious. He pinched himself to be sure he was awake and not dreaming.

They were going faster, turning left and right frequently, and for a moment, the labyrinth seemed endless. At one point, Andy asked the dwarves why there were so many turns and how long it would take to get to the end. Luscious was the first to respond, telling Andy,

"Master, this labyrinth has been designed for the village's safety. If you make a wrong turn, it takes you back to the beginning, and you'll have to start again." Moments later, Andy began to feel the rigors of the tunnel, and then this passage. So, he asked,

"Thaddeus, can we stop for a bit? I'm tired, and these shoes are a little small."

"Master, we're almost there. We can't stop now. If we do that, the bushes will start attacking us! Be strong. You can rest after we meet with Nikos."

"You're right; I can rest when we get there…"

"Only a few more turns, Master. We'll fix your shoes when we get to the village!" Thaddeus said.

Finally, they made the last turn, finding a green wall full of bushes. Andy, visibly disappointed, told the dwarves, "Oh God, we took the wrong turn. Now we have to start all over!"

"Don't be deceived by the appearance, Master!" Thaddeus replied, then pointed his right hand to the green wall of bushes and yelled: *Ludibikus out!*

The wall immediately opened, and there was the Dwarf Village, so colorful and full of flowers that it was hard to believe it was part of the same forest. As soon as they crossed the wall and reached the village, the people started greeting them warmly, not knowing who the human lad accompanying them was.

"Hello, Thaddeus… Luscious, welcome back!"

"Who is the lad with you? Someone we know?" a dwarf asked.

Luscious and Thaddeus returned the greetings, and Andy waved, saying hello to everybody. Suddenly, another dwarf, Vale, saw Andy and asked, "Luscious, Thaddeus! Is this the chosen one? The one marked by the clover?"

"The chosen one… The chosen one…" everyone around whispered.

Thaddeus calmly said, "Yes, he's the chosen one! We must see Nikos at once. He's expecting us."

It took a few seconds for the news to spread around the village. Many dwarves gathered around Nikos' cottage, yelling, "The chosen one has arrived!"

When Nikos heard that, he came out to see what was happening. When he stepped outside, he saw his two loyal friends, accompanied by a young human lad. His eyes glowed, and his heart pumped with joy.

"Welcome home, friends… Finally, we meet the chosen one! The Keymaster of the Golden Gate… well done!" Then, facing Andy, Nikos said, "Welcome, Sir Andy; we have been waiting for you for many years! Please, come inside my cottage and make yourself at home!"

Andy was impressed by the magnificent presence of Nikos, who had long white hair and a beard and was wearing an elegant robe. He stood in silence for a couple of seconds, thinking about what to say; then, the right words came to him at once,

"Thank you, Lord Nikos. It's an honor to be here. I don't know what I can do for this land, but I assure you I'll do my best."

Inside the cottage, they were served hot chocolate and some biscuits. Andy took his cup, and when he drank the first sip, he commented, "Hmmm… delicious. I've never had this kind of hot chocolate, and let me say that the one Mrs. Muller prepares at home is excellent, but this is unique. Is there something special in the flavor?"

"This is an old dwarf recipe. Hot chocolate is one of our specialties. It'll make you feel full of energy," Nikos told Andy.

The biscuits were delicious, for Andy was having a feast with them. When he ate the last one, Nikos told him,

"Sir Andy, you will rest now in the cabin we have especially prepared for you. Thaddeus told me about your shoes, so I'll fix them for you during your rest. This afternoon, we will teach you how to use them and the magic dust you need on your journey. We will have a little gathering celebrating your arrival tonight, but tomorrow, you will leave for the Forbidden Mountains at dawn. Now go and rest, Sir."

"Thank you for your hospitality, Lord Nikos… I'll see you later!"

Andy left Nikos' cabin, accompanied by Thaddeus and Luscious. Lumi directed them to the edge of the village, where the guest cabin was.

When they arrived at the cabin, Andy went directly to the large bed, specially built for him. Thaddeus told him, "Now rest, Master; the hot chocolate will help you to sleep, and you'll feel full of energy when you wake up. We'll be back… until then."

"Guys, don't leave me alone! Please!" Andy told the dwarves.

"Don't worry, Master; you'll be fine… we'll see you later!"

"Okay, guys. See you later," Andy responded as he yawned. He started feeling his eyes heavier and heavier, and in a few seconds, he fell asleep. Soon after, he began to have a fantastic dream. He didn't know that the biscuits were the reason for that.

In the dream, he was climbing a mountain when suddenly he heard a peculiar sound, like a strange voice. It seemed as though someone was in pain, and the sound grew louder as he neared the summit. When he finally reached the summit, the sound stopped. He looked at the other side of the mountain, which seemed deserted, with not a single plant or sign of life. All he could see was rocks, dirt, and dust.

Andy began to descend that part of the mountain, and when he was almost at the bottom, he saw the entrance to three caverns. When he got closer, he found two huge Panwolves (a giant beast with the body of a black panther and the head of a wolf) guarding the caves. He had never seen animals like these before. He quickly hid behind some rocks, but then, to his astonishment, he heard them talk.

"I'M SO HUNGRY THAT I COULD EAT ONE OF THOSE BIG RATS, KILA?"

"SHUT UP, BAKU! YOU KNOW THAT WE HAVE TO WAIT FOR OUR REPLACEMENTS TO MOVE FROM HERE! DON'T FORGET ZOLTAR'S ORDER!"

"BUT I CAN GO AND BRING ONE FOR BOTH OF US?"

"THERE ARE MANY THERE, BUT ALSO ARE SNAKES… AND THEY ARE HUNGRY, TOO! YOU WON'T SURVIVE!"

Andy was thinking: How do I pass those beasts? Do I use invisible dust? Maybe they can smell me. I can probably run faster than them, but in that tiny space, I need to either get them to move away or give them something to put them to sleep.

Then, Andy was awakened by a female voice.

"Master, wake up… wake up! Your lunch is ready."

"Ooh," Andy yawned and said, "Thank you; it's lunchtime already? How long have I been asleep?"

"Master, it is already past noon; thus, you have been sleeping for about four hours. Thaddeus and Luscious will be here in a few moments. Enjoy your food, sir!"

The lady dwarf was leaving Andy's cabin when his two friends came in, bringing Andy's shoes. Thaddeus, as usual, was the first to talk, asking Andy, "Master, did you sleep well? We have a busy afternoon ahead of us!"

"I'm glad to see you guys! I slept well, but I had a strange dream. I was climbing the mountain, and I came to the other side. There, everything looked like a desert. I found three caverns, and I figured one of them would take me to Henrietta… but guarding the entrance were two big animals I had never seen before. They were big and black, like panthers, but with the heads of wolves!"

"Master, the biscuits you ate have a special ingredient that makes you dream about the future. Right now, your future is going to that mountain and finding Henrietta. The animals you described are Panwolves, which live in the dark part of the forest. Zoltar used them to protect certain places and as hunters due to their high sense of smell…What else did you dream?"

"These two animals were talking. One told the other to go and hunt, but the other replied that they couldn't go anywhere. Zoltar's orders. Then, I thought the only way to pass would be to put them to sleep… then, that lady dwarf awakened me, and I couldn't see more."

"First of all, the Panwolves can't talk. Your imagination allows them to speak to you in your dreams, revealing what they want and how you can confront them. You'll need some of our sleeping potion. I'll tell Nikos to prepare something you can use on the Panwolves. Come, Master, finish your lunch. Nikos will be here soon to start your training."

"Wow, guys... Mmm! This is delicious! You have great food here! What do you call this?"

"This is our specialty. Ambrosia on the Rainbow."

"This is very good! By the way, the shoes are perfect now, and I feel great... That hot chocolate was the best one so far in my life!"

After Andy finished his lunch, Nikos came into the cabin.

"Bravo! You ate all your lunch, and you look much rested. Let me ask you, did you dream of something?"

"How do you know I had a dream, Lord Nikos?"

"Because you ate the biscuits," he retorted. "Now tell me... what did you see?"

Andy repeated to Nikos what he had told his two friends, and the dwarf lord responded very excitedly, "That's good, Sir Andy. We'll prepare some bits for you with the sleeping ingredient so you can give them to the Panwolves, but you still have to choose one of those caverns. Be wise, Sir Andy... and follow your guts. I know you'll choose the correct one! Now, let's go out to begin your training."

They looked for an open plain. Nikos wanted to train Andy to control the shoes and use the silver dust, so he brought a deer for the training.

Nikos told Andy, "Knock your heels once and start running." Andy did that, and he immediately started running fast. The deer was running, too, but faster than Andy. Then Nikos told him, "To stop, you have to point your right shoe gently against the ground, but with caution because if you do it too fast, you can Somers ---...."

Nikos didn't finish when Andy pointed his right shoe so fast that he somersaulted, falling on his back.

"Sault..." Nikos finished the sentence, but Andy was already lying on the floor, grabbing his back in pain.

Andy tried a few more times, but he fell several times until he started doing it better and better. "Okay, now knock your heels twice and run," Nikos yelled. Andy did it and began running, but he was faster than the deer this time.

"Remember how to stop! This time, you will fly if you do it too fast!" Nikos yelled.

But Andy did it perfectly, and he stopped without a problem. After a few more tries, Andy seemed to master how to use his shoes, so he was ready to run if the occasion arose. Next was the silver dust. Nikos explained to him how it worked and its temporary effects.

After a little break, Vale came to teach Andy how to use the dagger. He was the master dwarf in the use of weapons. So, before they start the training, he tells Andy, "All you need to do is wish where the dagger should go, and it'll obey."

They continued practicing for the rest of that afternoon. When they finally finished, Nikos told Andy, "Now, Sir Andy, go and refresh a little. We'll gather at the center of the village in an hour for a little feast! You've been an excellent disciple. Now you are ready; may the good faith go with you!"

Andy retired to his cabin to prepare for the small party in his honor, and about an hour later, the music began to sound, announcing the start of the feast; everyone in the village gathered at the center, ready to salute the chosen one.

When Andy came out of his cabin and saw all the dwarves waiting for him, applauding and cheering his name, he returned a warm smile in gratitude.

After Nikos gave him a proper welcome, they started the celebration. Everyone was dancing and singing, finally showing signs of hope. Andy still couldn't believe where he was; everything looked so unreal. He pinched himself again and realized he was living something real. He asked Nikos, "Lord Nikos, may I know who will be coming with me tomorrow?"

"Of course, Sir Andy, you'll be accompanied by Thaddeus, Luscious, and three of our best warriors, Vale, Kaleb, and Radu. They'll protect you with their lives, if necessary!"

"Thanks, Lord Nikos, it'll be an honor to go with them!"

Nikos ordered to stop the music and addressed his people, "Dear brothers and sisters, today we start a new era in our land. Hope and freedom are in our future, for we finally see the prophecy coming true. This Lad is the chosen one, and we'll do all we can to help him fulfill the prophecy and free this land from the evil Zoltar. Let's hear three hurrahs for our chosen one, Sir Andy!"

HIP, HIP HOORAY… HOORAY… HOORAY! Andy bowed in gratitude and told Lord Nikos, "It's time for me to retire. Tomorrow is an important day, and we should be ready early. I want to thank you for your friendship and hospitality. Good night!"

After Andy's words, the party officially finished, and everybody retired for the day. His two loyal friends escorted him to his cabin. This time, he looked more confident. Thus, he fell asleep quickly.

The following day, right at dawn, when Luscious and Thaddeus went to Andy's cabin to awaken him, they found him already awake, dressed, and in a great mood. "Good morning, Master," they said, and Andy responded, "Good morning, my friends. I'm ready, let's go."

"That's the right spirit, Master," Thaddeus said, and then they went to Nikos's cottage. In the dwarf Lord's cabin, they found the rest of the dwarves assigned to the mission. Nikos addressed the group, "Well, my friends, here are the bags with silver dust (Fedora had given him the formula to prepare more); four for each of you. Remember to use them only in extreme necessity and no more than two at a time. It's too dangerous to use more!"

Andy took his bags and said, "We'll be careful, Lord Nikos!"

"Good, Sir Andy." Then, Nikos added,

"I've something else for you, Sir Andy." He gave him a little wand, maybe no larger than 6 inches, saying, "This is a magic wand. It will give you light when you are in the dark; all you have to do is point it forward."

"Thank you, Lord Nikos," Andy replied, and Nikos, grabbing his own hands, said,

"Let's have a nice cup of chocolate before you go!"

Everyone was served hot chocolate and cookies. When they finished, Andy and the dwarves began their journey to the forbidden mountain, searching for Duchess Henrietta of Utopia and the ring of clovers...

Chapter Fourteen: The First Task

Andy and his friends were crossing the village, heading for the south corner to open the secret passage to the darkest part of the forest, which ends close to Forbidden Mountain, and from there goes to Death Mountain. Many dwarves were there, wishing them good luck. When they got in front of the entrance, Thaddeus moved his right hand and said the new password, *"Fidilikus in!"*

The wall of bushes opened, showing the new labyrinth. Thaddeus and Radu were the first to get in, followed by Andy, Luscious, Vale, and Kaleb.

Like in the first, they had to walk, turn in many directions, and be careful not to touch poisonous bushes.

After a few minutes, Andy broke the silence, asking, "Hey guys... why are you so quiet? Nobody has said a word since we've gotten into the labyrinth."

"Shhhhhh... Master, the bushes don't like to be disturbed. We'll talk when we finish crossing the passage!" Radu answered.

Almost one hour later, they reached the end of the labyrinth. Once again, Thaddeus said the password, *"Fidilikus Out."*

The green wall of bushes parted, revealing part of the Emerald Forest, which used to be one of the most beautiful, but now it looked like a horrific jungle.

They had to make their way through using hatchets to cut bushes full of thorns, and on top of that, there were fumes with a strong sulfur smell. Many plagues were sent to this area from Zoltar. Almost no life remained there, except maybe some snakes, spiders, wild rats, and Panwolves.

Then, Thaddeus told the group, "Radu and I will go ahead and check for any possible danger. Luscious, you will lead the second group, and the three of you will protect Andy at all costs. In any emergency, all of you must be ready to use the silver dust. Master, remember to use your magic shoes if needed, and Luscious, be ready to run with him; we don't want him to get lost. We will communicate using our flutes (Only dwarves can hear their special sound); one whistle means to take cover, and two to continue."

A Confused Andy asked Thaddeus, "Why will Luscious be the only one running with me? What about the others?"

"Because these shoes were made out of the skin of a panwolf, and we only had enough for two pairs, one for you and another for one of us, to go with you."

"I understand. I'll be ready!"

So, the group split in two, continuing their journey on high alert. The chance of encountering one of Zoltar's patrols was very high.

******

Meanwhile, Lucy talks to the two enchanted princes in the attic, telling them what she knows. Still amazed by all the events of that day, Danny had been asking Lucy to pinch him to be sure he wasn't dreaming.

Nolan and Morgana were surprised to hear their story and how they came to the other side of the world. Then, Nolan said,

"Lady Lucy… how will your brother find my aunt Henrietta after all these years? Only dwarves live that long, and of course, the evil Zoltar."

"We think the power of the ring must be keeping her alive. According to the prophecy, she's supposed to give it to the chosen one, my brother Andy!"

Danny was eager to participate in the conversation and said, "Your aunt has to be somewhere in that mountain. I'm sure Andy will find her!"

"We wish him the best of luck!" Morgana said in a soft tone.

******

At the Emerald Forest, Thaddeus and Radu were cutting bushes with their hatchets, opening their way through, when suddenly, they heard a rumbling noise that was getting closer. Thaddeus immediately took his flute and whistled once, alerting the second group to look for cover. Then he hid in the bushes with Radu. A group of trolls passed very close to them; six giant trolls, armed with large wooden clubs, made the ground tremble. They were going in the exact direction of the second group.

The second group also hid as soon as they heard the whistle. They were about one hundred yards behind the first group, and they felt the tremors, too. When the trolls drew closer to them, Andy looked at the beasts in absolute shock…he had only seen these kinds of monsters in fantasy books or movies, but what he had just seen was pretty amazing. These creatures were over eight feet tall with a grotesque appearance, long arms, large heads, and no hair; on top of that, they stank. Andy was about to puke when the patrol passed by him. After the trolls passed, he stood up immediately, and holding his nose, he told the dwarves, "Let's go, guys… I can't take this smell any longer." He almost barfed, and Luscious told him, "You better get used to it, Master; we'll see more of them anytime.

Andy nodded, and then he joined the rest of the second group to meet the first group. When they were there, Andy asked Thaddeus, "How far are we from the mountains?"

Thaddeus answered, "We should be there right before dark, Master."

"Are we going to encounter more patrols?" Andy curiously asked.

This time, Luscious responded, "Who knows? Maybe not if we follow the right path, but we must exercise extreme caution."

They continued their journey for a few hours, and thanks to the route they especially prepared, they didn't encounter any more patrols. But they had been walking through many bushes, foliage, and thorns, and were starting to feel the rigor of the march. Thaddeus ordered them to stop to get some rest and eat their rations, telling the group,

"We'll rest here for a little bit. Vale and Kaleb, you two prepare the fire and are the first to be on vigilance. Luscious and Radu will relieve you when they finish eating. Radu, get some water to prepare sopa (dwarf's soup). Master Andy, come and sit next to me!"

Andy seemed less tired than the others and started to look like a different person. He was eager to continue the journey and focused on finding Henrietta and the ring. His words were more assertive, as if he knew what to do.

After everybody had eaten biscuits and drank the soup, unexpectedly and for a reason he couldn't even fathom, Andy sensed something odd and told the dwarves, "I think someone is coming… Can you hear that?"

"No, Master, I don't hear anything," Luscious replied.

Andy stood up and, after a short pause, said, "It sounds like someone is running and growling. I can hear some animals too. They are getting closer to us, Vale; kill that fire! Everyone… get ready to use the silver dust!"

The dwarves stood up and got ready. Then, Andy told Luscious, "You and I will have to run now, but not too fast; I want those animals to follow us. We'll distract them so the others can use the silver dust to go directly to the mountain and meet us there."

"Master, I'm proud of you. You're acting more like our leader! Now I see why you are the chosen one… but how do you know someone is coming?" An excited Thaddeus said.

Before Andy could answer, Kaleb came running and yelling, "Patrol… Patrol! They have Panwolves!"

Without losing a moment, Andy grabbed Luscious and told him, "Follow me!" Then he said, "Thaddeus, we'll meet you at the end of the forest by the edge of the mountains. Good luck!" And they left in the direction of the patrol.

When they got the patrol's attention, there were four goblins and two Panwolves. One of the goblins ordered the others to release the Panwolves and attack Andy and the dwarf. Andy and Luscious looked at each other, and at the same time, they knocked on their heels and started running. The Panwolves were very fast and began to close in on them. Then Luscious gave Andy a signal to accelerate.

Thaddeus and the others used the silver dust so the goblins couldn't see them. Andy had been running as fast as he could, but a simple distraction caused him to trip over a bush. Thankfully, he did not get caught by a poisonous thorn. Luscious stopped and went on to help Andy, but the Panwolves were only seconds behind. Luscious asked Andy, "Are you okay, Master? We'll have to run faster now, or the Panwolves will catch us."

Andy, making an effort, stood up and knocked his heels twice simultaneously as Luscious. Just as the Panwolves were jumping to catch them, they disappeared, making the Panwolves bite only the bushes and get pricked by some thorns.

The patrol was far behind them, but the goblins already saw a human lad and a dwarf roaming in the forest. The goblins didn't know why they were there, but the news would reach Zoltar, and he would know that the dwarves were still alive and living in the forest.

Andy and Luscious continued running until they got closer to the mountains. Luscious stopped first; as expected, Andy completely forgot how to stop. As he was braking, he did it too quickly and flew at least ten feet ahead of Luscious, landing on his back... and close to a huge snake. When the snake was about to strike Andy, Luscious threw his dagger right at the snake's head, killing it instantly. Then Luscious told Andy, "Can you stand up, Master?"

"Yes, I can… I'm a little embarrassed, that's all!"

They walked a few steps and found a camp full of goblins and trolls guarding the mountain's entrance. So, pointing to a group of trees, Luscious told Andy, "Master, let's wait there for Thaddeus and the others."

"Okay," the boy replied.

Then Luscious asked him, "Master, how could you sense that patrol of goblins coming?"

"I don't know, but I heard them."

"Did you hear anything else, Master?"

"I could swear that I also heard a female voice humming. I'm not sure… it sounded far away!"

"I think we should mention this to Thaddeus. He may know why you heard that voice and then that patrol," Luscious replied. Then they found the bushiest tree, perfect for hiding under and waiting for the other group to arrive.

They waited almost half an hour until they finally spotted Radu, who was ahead of the group. Luscious played his flute and sent the signal to them. It was getting dark when they got together under that tree.

"I'm happy to see you again, guys!" Andy said.

"We're glad to see you, too, Master. Let's go to a better place so we can plan our next move. Nikos was right; there is a garrison of goblins and trolls protecting the entrance to the mountain; he mentioned to us before you came to his cabin…" Thaddeus said, and everyone moved a little closer to the camp. They didn't know that the patrol they had encountered earlier belonged to this camp and would be returning soon, reporting what they had seen in the forest.

Luscious approached Thaddeus and told him how Andy had sensed the patrol and the female voice he had heard before. After thinking for a minute, Thaddeus concluded,

"Master, the key is in the female voices you heard. The only ones capable of singing like that are the mermaids of the lake. They probably know you are in Ethernia, and when they sensed you were in danger, they sent you a message that only you could hear!"

"Wow, mermaids! Wait a second. How do they know I'm here, and how could they do that from so far away? I don't understand!"

"Master, remember that Fedora, their Queen, knew you were coming and could see you through the oracle and find your location in the forest. Mermaids have the power to make anyone they want listen to them. Remember, you could hear them even in your world. So, when they sent you that message, they improved your hearing abilities so you could hear the patrol coming!"

"That's weird, Thaddeus, because I can still hear the echo of that humming in my head!" Andy finally replied

Moments later, the same patrol they encountered was returning to the camp. Then, the lead goblin yelled to the goblin in charge, "We saw a dwarf in the forest, sir! He was with a human lad, but they ran too fast, and we couldn't catch them!"

"I'll send a message to Lord Zoltar; he believes all the dwarves are dead. He'll be very curious to find out where this one came from. I'll prepare our best hawk."

Andy and the dwarves were listening to the two goblins, and Thaddeus said, "This isn't good… if Zoltar knows about us, it could endanger the whole mission and, worse, the future of our people!"

"What are we going to do now?" Andy asked.

Thaddeus pulled Kaleb (who was a master archer) aside, gave him some silver dust, and told him, "Kaleb, you go and look for a good spot to stop that hawk; the goblins must not notice when you kill him; then go back to the village and tell Nikos what happened thus far. Remember, that hawk must not reach Zoltar, Understood?" Kaleb nodded in understanding and immediately left the group.

Moments later, when it got dark, the hawk left the camp carrying the message for Zoltar. The dwarves saw it in the distance, and Thaddeus said, "Kaleb is our only hope to stop that hawk; he must not fail."

Andy and the dwarves waited in the hide for a few hours until everybody in the camp was asleep. Only two trolls were guarding the front, each one with his Panwolf. Then, Thaddeus split the group in two and said, "Get your silver dust ready; Vale and I will go first and take care of the trolls, then we'll begin crossing the camp; Master Andy, Luscious, and Radu, you'll wait for my signal via flute and then start crossing the camp too, we'll meet again at the other side of the camp."

They knocked their heads with the little bags containing the silver dust, and seconds later, the five of them were invisible, except between them. So, as planned, Thaddeus and Vale moved quickly towards the first two guards. On their way, they took out their blowpipes and shot at the Panwolves and the guards with incredible aim, causing them to fall unconscious almost immediately. After pulling off the darts from their victims, they began crossing the camp.

Moments later, Andy, Luscious, and Radu received Thaddeus' signal and, without delay, began crossing the camp as fast as possible, although the smell was so awful they could hardly breathe. Thaddeus and Vale got to the end of the camp first and hid behind a group of rocks, waiting for the rest. A couple of minutes later, as Andy and the two dwarves approached the end of the camp, they unexpectedly found two more guards. Luscious and Radu quickly pulled out their blowpipes and shot the two guards with fantastic speed. Andy couldn't believe his own eyes; the two gigantic creatures collapsed in less than you count to three, and the two dwarves quickly pulled the darts off them.

Finally, the whole group met at the end of the camp, and Thaddeus whispered, "Let's go before somebody notices the guards are sleeping! We'll be visible again soon, so let's start climbing the mountain; we must reach the summit before dawn."

This mountain has three levels, and it would probably take them the rest of the night to reach the summit. Thaddeus led the group, and the rest were a few steps behind him. They began climbing that mountain using the moonlight as a guide. By then, they were already visible. When they reached the top of the first level, Andy asked the dwarves why they had to be at the summit before sunrise.

"Well, Master, let me put it this way: if we aren't there before sunrise, we may have to face all the creatures that live in the caverns of this mountain, like snakes, giant hawks, and the bats of the dark mountain. They're very dangerous," Thaddeus replied.

"In that case, we'd better hustle!" Andy yelled.

They continued to climb until they reached an area of the mountain with many caves. Thaddeus pointed the caves to the others, put his finger on his mouth, asked Andy and the others for silence, and whispered, "Any noise could wake up the creatures of these caves; let's keep quiet."

It was dark when they arrived at the third and final level, just before the summit. Suddenly, out of nowhere, two large hawks came out, flapping their wings. Thaddeus whispered to everyone to hide quickly between the rocks. When Andy saw the hawks, his eyes widened in amazement, for they were at least three times larger than any ordinary hawk.

"Did you see that? Those hawks are huge!"

"I think they didn't see us. Otherwise, they would have attacked us." Thaddeus retorted. They waited a few seconds, and after the hawks left the area, Andy and the dwarves continued their march.

Finally, almost at the stroke of dawn, the group arrived at the summit. They stopped to rest for a while, and Thaddeus told Andy, "Master, now you must continue alone. The death part of the mountain begins here; you must take the path down and look for the three caverns where Henrietta is a prisoner. Chances are, you won't face any hawks, but you may encounter some snakes. Be careful and have the silver dust ready. Remember your shoes and how to use your dagger. Also, here are some bits for the Panwolves guarding the three caverns. After you put them to sleep, remember to choose wisely. Follow your instinct and trust your heart; they will lead you to make the right choice."

"Well, my friends, I guess it's time for me to go. Don't worry, I'll be careful and bring Henrietta and the ring back! I'll see you later!"

"Goodbye, Master... and good luck!"

Then, Andy began his march down to the dead part of the mountain. He was scared but full of confidence and hope. This was the first step to fulfill the new prophecy...

Chapter Fifteen: A Wise Choice

Andy was descending the dead part of the mountain, and many things were passing through his already overwhelmed mind. Everything seemed like a dream to him: how he had come to be a part of this story and why he had been chosen for this task. He was also thinking about Lucy and Danny. What could have been happening to them in the attic when he suddenly thought, oh my God, my parents— they *probably noticed I'm missing by now*. He started to worry about that, but then he thought, *there is nothing I can do now. I'll deal with that when I return; maybe Nikos can help me. I have to focus on this task now.*

For a mysterious reason, clouds always covered the sun in this part of the mountain, making the days dark and gray. The surface was covered in dust and rocks, surrounded by holes from which fumes emanated. There was no sign of vegetation; the only life was some scorpions, snakes, and spiders.

When Andy finally reached the base of the mountain. He crossed paths with a Panwolf, which started to run towards him. Andy's mind blanked for a second; then, like a stroke of lightning, he reacted quickly by knocking his heels once and ran down to a hill full of large rocks and a couple of dead trees. That move confused the Panwolf, causing him to stop and wonder where Andy had gone.

Andy got to the hill and started to climb until he found a spot where he could have a good view of the three caverns and the Panwolves guarding them. He was about two hundred yards away. From there, he could see the two Panwolves very clearly. Then, he saw the one who chased him returning to the pack. For the next few minutes, he looked at them, studying their moves, and at the same time, he wondered which of the caverns could lead to Henrietta. He was waiting for the right moment to become invisible and set up the bits with the sleeping potion for the Panwolves.

Suddenly, he noticed that one of the Panwolves approached the one in front, exactly like it had happened in his dream. He thought, *now they are hungry. That is the one who wants to go hunting. I'll get closer and throw these bits. All it takes is one of them to come, and the others will follow.*

Andy knocked his head with the silver dust and turned invisible. He started approaching the caves very slowly and silently. When he was about one hundred feet from the Panwolves, he threw the bits as close to the Panwolves as possible. The hungry one heard the noise of the bits hitting the ground and came closer. The Panwolf took one and found it so delicious that he ate them all quickly. When the others saw this, they decided to get closer and try. Then Andy threw more bits for the other two, and the Panwolves ate them in seconds. The effects of the bits were strong, and the three Panwolves started collapsing one by one in seconds.

Without delay, Andy approached the caverns and began thinking: *Which one of these caverns is the one? I only have one shot. If I go in the wrong one, I'm doomed.*

Then he heard a little voice inside his mind repeating Nikos' words: "Trust your heart, and follow your instinct." Looking at the three caverns, he pointed at them, one at a time, and thought, *it couldn't be that easy... Eeny... meeny... miney... moe...*

He didn't finish saying that when he saw a small mark in the cave to the right. He got closer and saw a tiny little clover. Then, he realized the power of the ring of clovers had been protecting Henrietta for all these years. So, he said, "This has to be the one."

He entered the cave, and of course, it was utterly dark, so he pulled out the unique wand Nikos had given him for this occasion and pointed it forward. As he got deeper into the cave, he encountered a few rats and snakes, but he could quickly avoid them. After passing through a relatively narrow tunnel, he found a waterway inside the next cavern. It was about 30 feet wide, but the current was so strong that it would have been impossible to swim across without being dragged along. The question was how to reach the other side of the river… jumping seemed almost impossible.

An idea came to his mind in a flash, and he said, "I got it. I can use the shoes to give me enough impulse to jump to the other side!"

He backed up as far as he could, then hit his heels twice and started to run, picking up enough speed to jump to the other side of that narrow river, but he barely made it, and he had to make an effort to pull his feet out of the water to avoid being dragged by the current. When he stood up, he saw a black cat running away to a deeper part of the cavern. He ran after the cat and found a second tunnel. When he passed through it, he reached a small area that looked like a forest, and from there, he could see a cottage in the middle. The first thing that came to his mind was: *This is it; Henrietta has to be there.*

Andy saw the light inside as he approached the cabin, and his heart started beating faster. When he was about to look through the window, the same black cat he had just seen jumped over him, making him fall.

Then, standing over his chest, the cat said, "Who are you, and what do you want here?"

"**HOLY CRAP**! A talking cat!" Andy exclaimed.

"I'm not a cat. My name is Alina. Who are you?"

"Alina, oh yes, I remember now. Zoltar turned you into a cat. My name is Andy Logan, and I'm here to rescue Lady Henrietta and you!"

"**Andy, what?**" a horrible woman yelled, standing by the door of the cottage.

Ugly was a sweet way to describe this old woman's hideousness. Andy reacted with horror and repugnance. She was so ugly that a troll by her side looked like Prince Charming.

The cat moved off Andy's chest, and the woman asked, "Who are you, and who sent you?"

Andy tried to tolerate Henrietta's appearance and answered, "As I said, my name is Andy Logan. Lord Nikos sent me here to look for Lady Henrietta. I've got to take her with me with the ring of clovers. When I see her, I need to show her my birthmark."

When Andy was ready to show her his forearm, she interrupted, "You don't need to do that. Only the chosen one could come this far! I've always dreamed you were coming, but I never saw your face. Come inside, and we'll talk; I have some warm soup ready. By the way, I'm Lady Henrietta. Don't be deceived by my appearance."

Andy followed Henrietta to her cabin, still feeling a little confused. *I know Thaddeus told me that Henrietta had been turned into an ugly woman, but this one is beyond hideous. Let's see what she tells me he* was thinking.

When they got inside, she gave him a cup of a beverage. Andy hesitated, but looking at the woman's eyes, he saw something good about her and took it. After taking a sip, Andy asked her, "Excuse me, ma'am, but how do I know you are Lady Henrietta? I heard she was converted into a witch and sent to a cell in this mountain, but this house doesn't look like a cell, so how do I know you are her?"

"You will believe me when I give you the ring. It has been on my finger for many years… waiting for you!" the woman answered firmly.

She started pulling an ugly ring from her right hand. She had tried many times but could never pull it off. To her surprise, the ring came off her finger quickly and emitted an intense green light, making the old woman tremble and shake. The light was so intense that she and Andy both closed their eyes. When the light finally disappeared, Henrietta opened her left hand, and there it was, the beautiful ring of clovers. She said, "This ring belongs to you, young knight! It finally left my finger. Now it is your turn to wear it!"

Andy took the ring and put it on his finger. At that moment, he felt some energy passing through his body from head to toe, making him feel very confident and full of stamina. He took a deep breath and said, "Lady Henrietta, pardon my doubts; I should know it was you. We need to leave this place immediately before Zoltar knows I'm here. I must take you to the dwarf village; you'll be safe there!"

"Thank you, young man, but I can't leave this place. It's enchanted; every time I reach the tunnel, I get thrown back and can't move for almost half an hour!"

"There must be some way out. Otherwise, I won't be here; we have to try!" Andy said.

After finishing their beverages, Andy quickly told Henrietta about Nolan and Morgana and that they were safe in his house in the real world. She was confused and horrified by the news. Then Andy told her he'd explain in more detail later, but they didn't have much time. "We have to go now!" Andy said.

There was such a commanding tone in his voice that Henrietta followed him without hesitation. She put a few things in a bag and told the cat, "It's time to go, Alina; this young lad will take us out of here. Come on!"

They doused the fire, and Andy, offering his hand, invited Henrietta to leave the place. When they left the cottage, something odd happened with the ring. Andy felt his finger burning, so he immediately removed the ring and noticed something shining inside. It was an inscription that read.

"Blow through the ring and call Cyclos…"

"That's it. The ring is telling us how to get out! Get closer to me, Lady Henrietta, and you, Alina… come into my arms!"

They were facing the tunnel. Andy was holding the cat in one arm with Henrietta beside him. Then, with the other hand, he put the ring facing his mouth, blew through it, and yelled, **"Cyclos!"**

A small twister began to form around them, and in a matter of seconds, it took them through the tunnel and the cavern, throwing them outside, right in front of the sleeping Panwolves.

Andy turned to see how Henrietta and the cat were and couldn't believe his eyes. She was still ugly, but no longer disgusting and horrific. He told them, "Lady Henrietta, you look different. I think the spell is getting weaker. Alina, are you okay?"

"Of course, I'm okay!" the cat responded.

"Well, let's go now before these creatures wake up. Alina, can you go in front and tell us if you see any danger?"

The lad and the old woman started climbing the dead side of the mountain back to the summit. It was already dark, so they were going as fast as they could. However, Henrietta started feeling the rigor of the climbing and asked Andy to stop so she could rest. After a few minutes, they continued at a much slower pace since that part of the mountain was steeper, demanding a more considerable effort from Henrietta. When they were about to take a second rest, a snake appeared out of nowhere. Andy immediately drew his dagger and engaged the snake, throwing it with fantastic skill, burying it right in the middle of the snake's head, killing the beast instantly.

Henrietta opened her eyes in admiration and said, "Sir, you are truly a brave man for such a young age. The dwarves have taught you well."

Thank you, my lady. Your words are very kind, but this is a magic dagger, and all I have to do is choose the target, and she will do the rest."

"Still, it takes a lot of guts to face a snake. Don't diminish your courage!" Henrietta said.

"Thanks again," Andy said, thinking *she sounded like my mother*. "Let's go now. We must be at the summit before sunrise to avoid any other attacks. We'll rest up there."

So, they kept going, but in the darkness of the night, they did not notice that Henrietta was changing little by little back to her usual self. Of course, this made her feel strong and able to continue climbing. When they were closer to the summit, Andy told Henrietta, "Let's stop here to get something to eat; this will give us the energy to continue. We're getting closer to the summit."

He pulled a couple of biscuits from his bag and gave them to Henrietta, along with a little piece for the cat.

They finally arrived at the summit with the first light of dawn. Andy, who was ahead, turned to help Henrietta, and when he saw her face again, he couldn't believe how much she had been changing throughout the night. Her repulsive aspect was gone. She looked almost like her old self. "Oh, my God! You're looking almost normal again, ma'am!" Andy said.

She touched her face and looked at her arms and hands. She couldn't believe it either, so she gave Andy a big hug of gratitude, saying, "Thank you, young knight; it has been so long. Thank you very much."

When they turned to the other side of the mountain, they found the group of dwarves waiting for them; Thaddeus saw them and yelled,

"Master Andy, welcome back! Ah… Lady Henrietta, it's indeed so nice to see you too."

The four dwarves bowed to Lady Henrietta and approached Andy to give him a welcoming hug.

"Bravo, Master, bravo! You did it! You rescued her!" Luscious yelled.

Thaddeus noticed the ring in Andy's hand and said, "Well done, Master; you have the ring of clovers, too. We must reach the village as soon as we can. Every moment counts. As long as we're here, we are in imminent danger…"

"You're right, Thaddeus, but we're tired. Let's rest at least a few minutes, for Henrietta!"

You're right, Master. We'll give some time to Lady Henrietta to rest and for you, too, Master."

About one hour later, they began to descend the mountain. They had to be extra careful to avoid the creatures of the mountain and needed to figure out how to cross the camp once more. Suddenly, Andy remembered something he had on his mind before and asked Thaddeus with great concern,

"Thaddeus, I've been in Ethernia for almost three days already. By now, my parents should know I'm missing and must be looking all over for me. Lucy and Danny should be in huge trouble."

"Master, don't worry! For them, it has been only a few hours."

"Give me a break… a few hours only? That's impossible. Three days have passed since we came." Then Andy saw Thaddeus' face and decided not to argue anymore.

They continued descending the mountain, and for some reason, they couldn't fathom, their path was free of any danger, like some force was protecting them.

When they got closer to the camp of goblins and trolls, they stopped at a prudent distance and waited there for the night, to cross it again. The fastest way to reach the forest was to cross right through the middle of the camp; otherwise, they would have to go around and through a rocky area, which would take them longer.

Later, when all the camp's lights finally went off, and with the help of the silver dust, the four dwarves, Andy, Henrietta, and the cat, started to cross it. They split into three groups to facilitate the crossing. Thaddeus and Andy went first, Luscious with Henrietta a few yards behind, and finally Radu and Vale, with the cat at the end.

It took them a few minutes to cross that filthy and nasty camp. All of them were holding their breaths, including the cat, and walking on their toes so as not to make any noise. When they were about to reach the end of the camp, Vale stepped on a little branch, and the noise caught the attention of one of the guards, who came in their direction to see what had caused that noise. Vale ran to the bushes and entered the forest, but the guard saw the bushes moving and called the other guard.

He pointed at the bushes and said, "Hey, Tandor, come quickly; I think I saw something moving in those bushes."

"Relax, Flukar, it could be a small animal! Don't worry; who would be so stupid to come closer to this camp?"

"Yeah, but let me check anyway." The guard came closer to the bushes as Andy and the dwarves were holding their breath. Since he couldn't see a thing, he told the other, "You're right, Tandor. There's nothing here. Let's finish our round and then drink some Bere" (the Favorite Goblin and Troll beverage).

The guards returned to their post, and Thaddeus told the others, "We're lucky we have the silver dust. Otherwise, we'd be in trouble. Let's go now before we turn visible again." After that scary moment, they began crossing the forest. Thaddeus, of course, was at the front; Andy was with Henrietta behind him, and the others were further back. About one hour later, Andy asked Thaddeus if they could stop to give Henrietta some rest, and Thaddeus responded, "Master, we have to continue. The gate to the passage will appear at the highest point of the moon soon after midnight and will be there for only one hour. If we miss it, we'll have to wait until tomorrow morning. In broad daylight, it could be dangerous for us. Remember, we don't have any silver dust anymore!" Then, Andy turned to Henrietta and asked, "Can you continue, ma'am?"

"Yes, don't worry about me. I've been waiting long enough for this moment!" she said. The beautiful moonlight allowed Andy to see her face again, and he was stunned. Henrietta looked almost as she was before the enchantment. The farther she was away from the mountain, the weaker the spell became.

Moments later, they arrived at the entrance to the passage. It looked like an ordinary bush, but Thaddeus knew better, and once again, he moved his right hand and said, *"Fidilikus in!"*

The bush opened like a gate, showing the green labyrinth that would take them back to the dwarf village. Thaddeus said to the group, "One at a time! Remember, don't touch the bushes, and be silent. We'll be there soon!"

They entered the labyrinth one by one, hungry and tired but finally free of any danger, at least for now. They would be in the dwarf village soon enough to enjoy the moment with Nikos and the whole dwarf nation. The first challenge was completed…

Chapter Sixteen: Aurus Wind

Andy, Henrietta, and the dwarves were walking in the labyrinth. They all looked tired, but their expression was hopeful and satisfied; the first challenge had been completed. In his mind, Andy recalled all the events of the last three days, but everything still seemed like a dream. He couldn't wait to go home and tell Lucy and Danny everything that happened to him during his first visit to Ethernia.

Almost at the end of the labyrinth, Andy turned to see how Henrietta was doing, and once again, he was stunned to see her transformation. She looked almost as she had before the spell.

When she looked at him, she smiled with gratitude.

Andy held her hand and asked, "Are you okay, ma'am? We're almost there!"

"Thank you, Sir Andy; I'm okay and very grateful to you and the dwarves!"

"No need to thank me, ma'am; it has been an honor!"

"SHHH... remember the bushes!" Luscious said to them.

It was almost dawn, and our friends were at the end of the labyrinth. Thaddeus approached the green wall and said the password, *"Fidilikus out!"*

The green wall opened, revealing the dwarf village and a vast reception committee. Nikos presided, and Kaleb was there, too. When they cleared out of the labyrinth, an explosion of jubilation erupted everywhere. Many dwarves surrounded Andy and cheered him. The others made references to Lady Henrietta.

She responded by removing her hood and nodding in gratitude to the dwarves. Everyone there expected to see a horrible witch. Instead, they were stunned to see a beautiful woman; her hair was still a little gray, and her face had a few wrinkles. Nikos was the first to speak. "Lady Henrietta, it's a great honor having you with us and seeing that you are no longer the horrible creature we heard you were converted into. How is this possible?"

"Nikos, old friend, I don't know. I believe the power of the ring of clovers and being as far away as possible from that mountain may have weakened Zoltar's spell."

"Lady Henrietta, here you will be safe. Consider this village as your home!"

"Thank you, Lord Nikos, but my main concern is to help Nolan and Morgana."

"We don't know that yet, my lady, so we must be patient. Fedora needs to know about the success of this first challenge so she can consult the oracle and find out what to do next."

"Believe me, Nikos, all those years on that mountain have taught me patience!"

"Good! Now, you will rest, and later, we'll have lunch in the main house with Master Andy before he returns to his world!"

Andy was still with the dwarves, getting hugs and low-fives (high for the dwarves), when he was called by Nikos, who told him,

"Well done, Sir Andy! I couldn't be prouder of you. The people of Ethernia are very grateful to you!"

"Lord Nikos, it was an amazing experience. I'm looking forward to the next challenge!"

"Easy, Sir Andy, you'll have time for that! Now go to rest; we're having lunch in the main cabin before you return home."

Andy and Henrietta were escorted to their cabins, where they rested for a few hours before going to the dwarves' main house for lunch. When Henrietta awoke, Lumi was there with a set of clothes, some makeup, and a mirror. So, after helping her to get dressed and look her best, Lumi said, "Oh, my lady, please, look at yourself!"

She gave her the mirror, and when Henrietta saw her face, she began to cry. She was completely back to normal.

"Oh, Lumi, look at me. It's me again. I've been waiting for so long to be able to see my real face again! Thank you very much!"

"No need to thank me, ma'am; I didn't do anything!" Lumi told her.

Meanwhile, Andy and the rest of the dwarves were gathered at the main cabin. Andy received a new set of clothes for the occasion, and he was seated between his two loyal friends, Thaddeus and Luscious.

Everyone was talking and laughing. Suddenly, Lumi interrupted, saying, "Good afternoon, everyone. Allow me to present the grand duchess, Henrietta of Utopia!"

Henrietta made her entrance, receiving a big "wow" from everyone. They couldn't take their eyes off her, as she was ultimately back to normal. After bowing to Nikos, everyone gave her a standing ovation. She was once again the beautiful woman she had been before the spell.

"Lady Henrietta, you look beautiful. It's great to see you back to yourself. In the name of all the dwarf people, I want to give you our most cordial welcome, and from now on, you're our guest of honor!"

"Thank you very much to you and your people, old friend. I don't have words to express my gratitude to this brave young man for rescuing me and bringing me safely here. It's indeed a privilege to be your guest. I hope we can do the same with my nephew Nolan and Princess Morgana and free this land from the evil Zoltar!"

Pointing at Andy, Nikos replied, "My lady, you can be sure of that. We have waited many years for this young man to arrive, and I believe he has proven so far that he is the chosen one who will help us free this land. Now, I want everyone to enjoy this feast that was specially prepared in your honor and Sir Andy's!"

Following Nikos' words, everyone continued with the feast, enjoying the food and drinks. Andy spent most of the time telling a group of dwarves (including Thaddeus and Luscious) about his experience walking down Death Mountain, how he chose the proper cavern, and how he and Henrietta managed to escape.

Meanwhile, Lumi was giving the cat (Alina) a delicious treat, and the cat said,

"At least the Lady went back to normal; now I have to wait for my turn."

"I'm sure Sir Andy and the rest will find a way to help you get back to normal."

Henrietta was telling Nikos about her horrible life as a prisoner of that mountain, forced to eat frogs, rats, and snakes without seeing daylight. When she finished, still confused by the whole experience, she asked the lord dwarf, "Lord Nikos, I lost all sense of time. Could you tell me how long I've been on that mountain?"

"You were frozen in time for many years, helped by the power of the ring of clovers. Many generations have passed in Ethernia, my lady. From your time, only Zoltar and the dwarves are still alive because, for us, time passes in another way. What he doesn't know is that we're still here. He believes we were exterminated, with all the plagues he sent to the forest throughout the years; he doesn't know that we've been hiding our village all this time. He'll know very soon that you have been freed, and we must be prepared for his reaction. Time is now running normally for you."

When lunch ended, Nikos stood up and addressed the people in the room: "My lady, Sir Andy, and friends… We must now say goodbye to our young Knight. He must return to his world and await the next challenge. I'll send a messenger to the Lake to inform Fedora that the first task has been accomplished. She'll tell us what to do next. Sir Andy, you'll have to take the ring with you. You're now the bearer and protector of it. In a short time, Thaddeus and Luscious will visit you and tell you what to do next. We want to thank you once again for helping us."

"You're welcome, Lord Nikos! I'm looking forward to my return, but let me ask you, how am I going to explain this ring to my parents? Wearing it will raise too many questions!"

"You can hide it when you're back in your world. However, in Ethernia, you ought to wear it at all times. Now, you have to go to the north passage; it will take you to the portal to your world. You need to get there before dark; Thaddeus will tell you what to do when you get there."

After saying goodbye to all his new friends, including Lady Henrietta, Andy departed from the dwarf main cabin, accompanied by Luscious and Thaddeus. As they walked to the north passage, the whole village followed them. When they finally reached the entrance, Andy turned and waved to everyone, saying, "Goodbye!"

Then, he turned around and faced the green wall when Thaddeus yelled the new password: *"Nordialikus in!"*

The green wall opened, revealing the north side labyrinth, and our friends entered one by one, with Thaddeus at the front, followed by Andy and Luscious, who crossed the gate behind him.

They walked through the labyrinth in complete silence. No one said a word so as not to disturb the bushes. *How long will it be until we see each other again?* They were thinking. Andy was also anxious to get home and tell Lucy and Danny about his fantastic experience in Ethernia.

When they reached the end, Thaddeus stood, facing the green wall, and yelled, *"Nordialikus Out!"*

Once again, the green wall opened, showing the north side of the forest. They were only moments away from the entrance to the tunnel that would take Andy back to the golden door in the attic. Then, Andy broke the silence, telling his friends, "I'm going to miss you guys! How long will it be until I see you again?"

"We'll return as soon as we know the next task, and don't be sad; we'll miss you too!"

They continued to walk until they saw a sign in the shape of a twister on a tree. Thaddeus gave a signal to stop there and told Andy,

"Master, I'll say the magic word, and you'll have to jump into the little twister. It'll take you to the tunnel; you must go alone this time. Remember, lock the door again when you get to your attic!"

"What happens if Lucy and Danny aren't there?"

"Don't worry, Master; they're still there but probably sleeping. Remember that, for them, it's been only a few hours. Now, Master, I need you to get the golden key and raise your hand, pointing to the sky!"

When Andy raised his hand with the key, Thaddeus yelled, *"AURUS WIND… AURUS WIND… COME TO PICK UP THE GOLDEN KEY!"*

A few seconds later, a little twister appeared only a few feet from Andy, and the dwarves yelled to him, "Master, you have to jump… Now!"

"What?! Jump in there?" Andy replied, a little confused.

"Don't be afraid, Master. That's your way back to the tunnel! Goodbye, and see you soon!"

"Goodbye, guys. See you soon!"

Andy jumped into the twister and disappeared almost instantly. A few seconds later, everything went dark, and he was softly thrown inside the tunnel and back to the golden door. All he could see was a little light at the top of it, so he began to climb, knowing that on the other side of that light was his home, where Danny and Lucy were waiting for him.

He knew they probably wouldn't believe what had happened to him, considering he had been in Ethernia for four days, and only a few hours had passed for them. His heart was beating a little faster as he was getting closer.

The light at the end looked bigger and bigger, and now he could see the portal to the other side of the golden door. He was so close that he began straightening his arm to touch the doorknob. He could feel it now. He grabbed it and turned the knob, opening the door, and then there he was, back in the attic.

Lucy and Danny were sleeping, leaning their heads on their arms on the table. The Music Box was open right by their side. Andy was finally home… He stepped inside the attic, thinking about how he would explain that he had done what he did in only a few hours for them.

When he closed the door, Lucy and Danny woke up, and after a smile of relief, the three of them embraced in a long hug. They laughed for a few seconds, but they had many questions to be answered…

Chapter Seventeen: The Wrath of Zoltar

"Welcome back, kid brother! We're happy to see you. But how come you're back so soon? You only left a few hours ago; did you rescue that lady?" Lucy asked Andy, anxious to know.

"So good to see you, sis, and yes, I did it, but there's so much to tell you; I don't know where to start, and I don't know if you'll believe me."

"Wait, before you start, you must see something, Andy! You're not going to believe this…" Lucy told him.

She pointed at the music box and called, "Princess Morgana, Prince Nolan! I want you to meet my brother Andy."

"What?" Andy exclaimed.

He was staring at the two little people inside the music box that bowed at him.

"Sir, I'm delighted to make your acquaintance. Your sister already told us what you are doing for our land. We are deeply grateful!" Nolan said.

Holy crap... The dolls are talking! He thought briefly and then reacted, "I beg your pardon; the pleasure is all mine. But, tell me… how come you two are alive in that box?"

"We don't have any idea, young sir; all we know is that we just came back and can't go out of this box," Nolan said.

"I'll ask the dwarves about this. Surely, they know why this is happening, or maybe Zoltar's power is weakening after all," Andy added. "I have to tell you about your Aunt Henrietta, and, most importantly, I have the ring of clover with me." He showed the ring to everyone, including the tiny prince and princess.

"So that's the famous ring! Wow... that's awesome!" Danny stated.

"Well, guys, let me start by telling you something... chances are you won't believe this, but I've been in Ethernia for the past four days and..."

"That's impossible! What do you mean four days?!" Danny exclaimed. "We've been here all the time, and it's almost 3:00 a.m.! You left just minutes before 11:00. I'm not a genius, but that's only four hours!"

"Yes, Danny is right; we've been here the whole time. How come you're saying that you spend four days in Ethernia?" Lucy added.

"How can I explain this... mmm...I don't understand this too well either; the dwarves told me that an imbalance was created when crossing this gate to Ethernia, resulting in two different sets of time. I guess that's why I spent four days in Ethernia, but only four hours have passed here."

"That's awesome, man! So, tell us, what happened?" Danny asked.

Andy began by describing day by day, event by event, the rescue of Henrietta in the Dead Mountain, his encounter with the trolls, the goblin and troll camp, the dwarf village, the magic shoes, and so on, having the absolute attention of everyone in the room, including the prince and princess.

They were so engrossed in the story that they lost track of time. It was already past six o'clock in the morning, and the first lights of the new day were starting to show. Suddenly, the prince and princess moved to the center of the music box, facing each other, and entered their enchanted position as sunlight poured in through the attic window.

Andy was the first to notice it and said, "Guys, did you see that? They're frozen again. It must be the daylight. Maybe when we opened the golden door, some counter-spell affected the music box to make them come alive, but only for the night. We'll confirm it tomorrow, or if it only happens when we open the gate. I hope the dwarves come soon so I can ask them!"

Then, Lucy interrupted him.

"Andy, it's almost daylight. Let's put everything in its place and go to our rooms before Mom and Dad wake up. We can meet later and continue our conversation!"

So, they put everything back in the attic and returned to their rooms. Andy and Danny went to the kitchen first to put the key to the attic back in the cabinet.

Andy hid the ring in a safe place inside his closet, and then the two youths went to bed and fell asleep almost instantly. They were so tired that they slept almost until noon that day.

Danny was the first to awake, and he said to Andy, "Dude, are you awake?"

"Groan," Andy replied.

"Dude, it's almost noon. Wake up!" Danny insisted.

Andy jumped from the bed and said, "Oh, Crap! It's so late, we have to go downstairs... now!

They went down for breakfast, and when they got to the kitchen, Mrs. Muller gave them a nasty welcome, complaining about why they had come so late for breakfast. So, without saying a word, they took a ball with cereal and returned to Andy's room. Everything was normal in Logan's house except for one thing: the three youths were now involved in this fantastic and magical adventure.

After lunch, the three gathered at Andy's and promised to keep this an absolute secret. Then Danny went home, and the siblings returned to the usual routine. Later that night, they returned to the attic to check on the music box and see if anything had happened to the prince and princess. However, after waiting for more than an hour, nothing had changed, and they eventually returned to their rooms.

******

At the Emerald Forest, Nikos ordered the council to relocate their village and sent Kaleb and Vale to inform Fedora of the news. He was sure it would be a matter of time before Zoltar discovered that Henrietta had escaped, and it would be unsafe to keep the village in that location.

That morning at the dark castle, Zoltar felt uneasy. It was too quiet and peaceful, and he didn't like that at all. He decided to send Simon to the mountains to check if everything was under control.

"Simon, I want you to go and check the Dead Mountain. Take one of the dragons and see if everything is okay. Then, go to Utopia and see that Morton is collecting all the taxes…"

"As you wish, Master, but I think there's nothing to worry about; that old woman can't take one step out of that cave, and even if she could, the Panwolves would have taken care of her!"

"Go now, Simon! I need to know that everything is fine. You know the rumors about that chosen one who will come to defy me; people have been talking about that for generations!"

"They're only rumors, Master; no one in this land can defy you. Whoever tries will be a dead person, and they know it!"

"Yes… you're right, Simon. Now go, and inform me as soon as you confirm everything is under control. Send me a message if something is amiss."

"Yes, Master, I will!"

Simon left the castle, took one of the two remaining dragons he had (he had been raising dragons since Zoltar took power, but they were affected by his plagues and were almost extinct), and flew straight to the mountains.

By then, Vale and Kaleb had arrived at the lake and, using the secret shells, sent a signal underwater. They waited a while before one of the messengers came to the surface; it was Lorain, the mermaid. They gave her the message from Nikos, and before swimming back to the bottom of the lake, she told them to wait for the Queen's answer.

Flying at a fast speed, Simon and the dragon were approaching the Goblin's Camp. One of the guards saw him coming and immediately notified their captain, who ordered a formation to honor the visitor.

When Simon landed, he told the captain, "I expect everything is under control, and there's nothing to report, Captain Nasu?"

"Sir, I thought you came in answer to our message!"

"What message? We never received any messages!"

"But, sir, we sent our top hawk a couple of days ago because we saw a dwarf in the forest, accompanied by a human boy."

"And you captured them, I suppose?"

"No, sir; they were using some kind of magic shoes, and they ran very fast, disappearing from our reach!"

"Are you sure they were alone?"

"That's affirmative, sir. They are probably hidden somewhere in the forest. I've sent several patrols to look for them!"

"I need to go to the Dead Mountain; Lord Zoltar is waiting for my report, and he won't like to know that a dwarf and a boy are loose in the forest!"

Simon immediately hopped on top of the dragon and flew to the death side of the mountain. When he arrived at the three caverns, the Panwolves were there guarding the entrance like nothing had happened. These beasts feared dragons and moved aside to let the dragon land. Simon got off the dragon and entered the cave.

Upon arrival at Henrietta's place, he went directly to the cottage and found no one inside. He searched everywhere and could not even find a single hair of the cat (Alina). *How am I going to tell the Master about all this? On top of that, the finding of the dwarf with the lad in the forest? He is going to be extremely upset.* He though

Simon left the cavern so furious and, without delay, jumped on top of the dragon and returned to the camp. He thought somebody had to pay for this, and it wouldn't be him. When he landed in the camp again, he called the captain.

"Captain Nasu, Captain Nasu! The prisoner has escaped! Somebody has broken through this camp. You'd better have a good explanation for this. Otherwise, Lord Zoltar won't show mercy for you or your soldiers!"

"My Lord Simon, I can assure you that nobody has crossed the camp. I don't understand; we always have guards on duty!"

"You better call those guards now; I want to talk to them." Then he thought, *I better send a message to Lord Zoltar.*

After sending the Dragon with the message to Zoltar, Simon and Captain Nasu interrogated the guards who had been on duty for the last few days, but none of them saw anything to report.

******

By then, at the lake, the mermaid Lorain was giving Vale and Kaleb the following message from Fedora, "Our queen said she has been consulting the oracle, and she'll see Nikos upon the next full moon to tell him what to do next."

Our two little friends returned to the village as fast as they could, taking that critical message to Nikos.

******

The dragon flew over the Emerald Forest carrying the message that would make Zoltar utterly furious. Henrietta was free, but most importantly, the ring of clovers was out of Zoltar's control, and to make matters worse, a dwarf had been seen in the forest accompanied by a young human.

When the dragon arrived at the castle, a guard took the message and gave it to Zoltar, who read it and reacted by killing that guard. He immediately went so mad that his face turned beet red; he raised his arms and yelled so loud that a dark cloud covered the entire city, and lightning flashed in the sky, followed by rolling thunder. He immediately hopped on the dragon and ordered it to fly to the mountains. He wanted to see for himself what had just happened there. His eyes were full of wrath.

Chapter Eighteen: The Eye of the Seeker

The Dragon carrying Zoltar flew so fast that it looked like a fireball hurtling through the sky. It only took them a few minutes to cross the Emerald Forest. They even passed close to the dwarf village, where many thought it was a shooting star, but Nikos felt so uneasy that his first thought was that this had something to do with Zoltar. He was waiting for the messengers to arrive from the lake to move the village again.

In the meantime, Vale and Kaleb were already in the secret passage, heading for their village. They were almost running, knowing the importance of the message, and they wanted to deliver it as soon as possible.

******

At the camp, Simon and the soon-to-be-fried Captain Nasu were waiting along with the garrison of goblins and trolls, and the tension was high. They knew how cruel Zoltar could be when he was upset… and he was not only upset, he was furious, and someone had to pay for that.

Moments later, the fireball appeared right on top of the camp, and to everyone's astonishment, there he was, Lord Zoltar, seated on the dragon, landing right in front of them.

When Zoltar set foot on land, everyone bowed to him, and Simon approached him and whispered, "Welcome, Master. Did you have a… Pleas-" Before he finished, Zoltar yelled at him.

"Shut up, you idiot! What's the meaning of this note you sent me? And where's the captain of this camp?!"

"Yes, my lord. I am Captain Nasu. I can assure you that we never saw any-" Before he finished, Zoltar sent a ball of fire, which fried the poor captain in seconds, burning him like charcoal on a barbecue grill. Everyone else was looking in panic.

Then, Zoltar ordered Simon, "Come with me, now; we're going to the Dead Mountain. I want to see for myself what happened!" Looking at the goblin that was behind the 'extra crispy' Captain Nasu, he said,

"You! What's your name?"

"Lieutenant Moko."

"You're in command now.

"The guards are waiting to be questioned, my lord!" the goblin answered.

Zoltar and Simon hopped on the dragon and flew to the dead side of the mountain. The Evil lord was about to confirm that his long-time prisoner had just escaped without leaving a clue of her new whereabouts.

When the evil lord and Simon arrived at the long-time prison of Henrietta and found the cottage empty, a sudden feeling of nausea invaded Zoltar's body. He looked at Simon and bit his lip, trying to contain himself so he would not give him the same treatment as Captain Nasu. After a long pause, in which Simon held his breath, Zoltar looked at the top of the cavern and released such a strong yell that it made the whole mountain tremble, scaring even the rats and bats, which stampeded out of the three caverns.

At that moment, luck smiled at Simon when he discovered two different sets of footprints outside the cottage and showed them to his master, saying,

"Someone helped the old witch to escape, master." And Zoltar responded, "That someone not only passed through the camp but also these stupid Panwolves."

On their way out of the cave, Zoltar snapped his fingers, turning the Panwolves into chickens, which the dragon devoured in seconds. Simon was speechless to see that demonstration of power and didn't dare to comment.

At the camp, all the guards on duty for the last four nights were waiting in formation for Zoltar's unmerciful judgment. When he returned, the evil lord approached the formation and yelled, "Porkus Convertus" without blinking, turning all the guards into warthogs. Looking at the cage full of Panwolves, he waved his right hand and freed them, ordering them to hunt the warthogs.

Everyone in the camp was utterly quiet; no one dared to look Zoltar in the eyes, fearing who would be the next to be punished. Then, he ordered Simon to begin the search for Henrietta, the dwarf, and the human lad. "Send everybody to find that human boy and the dwarf. You are personally responsible, Simon, and this time, I won't tolerate any failure; do you understand?" Simon nodded and replied, "Yes, Master."

Then, Zoltar took the dragon, and after telling Simon that he'd send the dragon back so Simon could go to Utopia, he returned to his castle in Ambrosia. Simon, visibly scared, called Lieutenant Moko and said,

"Moko, you heard the master; send patrols to the forest. That dwarf and the boy have to be found. I don't want to hear any excuses!"

"Yes, my lord Simon; Understood…"

By then, at the dwarf village, Vale and Kaleb had just arrived and went directly to the main cabin, where Nikos and the council were waiting for them to receive Fedora's message. Kaleb told them, "Lord Nikos, you must see the Queen on the next full moon. By then, she'll have the next task for the Keymaster." As soon as Kaleb finished, Nikos and the council began the ritual to relocate the village.

******

That night, Andy and Lucy returned to the attic to check on the music box, but they found the dolls precisely as they had the first time: enchanted and with no signs of life. They checked again for the next two nights with the same results. Finally, they concluded it was probably a counterspell produced by opening the Golden Gate.

After the Christmas vacation, the three youths continued with their everyday lives. Lucy returned to college, and Andy and Danny went back to school. For the next few weeks, they didn't have any news from the dwarves, and every day seemed like an eternity without knowing what would happen next.

******

At Ethernia, things got even worse when Zoltar ordered every citizen to be questioned about the new prophecy or whether they knew anything about the dwarves. No one could leave their home without fear of being interrogated and tortured. Zoltar was on a mission to find Henrietta and that mysterious boy at any cost.

A new full moon and a new trip to the lake by Nikos to meet Fedora and find out the next task for the Keymaster. The journey wouldn't be easy; the forest was full of patrols with orders to arrest any human or dwarf on sight and kill them if they resisted.

Nikos chose only five men to go with him (Radu, Vale, Kaleb, and our two friends, Thaddeus and Luscious) and prepared a route that included the use of multiple passages to get to the lake; the parts of the open forest would have to be crossed at night and using the silver dust, to be protected against any of Zoltar's patrols.

Late that afternoon, the dwarves left the village and opened the first passage, using the new magic words, *"Aburealikus in."* They crossed the labyrinth, calculating to be at the exit right after dark.

When the group exited the passage, Nikos ordered them to use the silver dust. But before they could apply it, the ground began to rumble, announcing that a patrol was approaching. Nikos signaled to the others to quickly hide in the foliage and not make any move or noise. Seconds later, the patrol passed, almost running, and the dwarves held their breaths. Even though the Panwolves seemed to look in their direction, they continued running with the patrol.

After they put on the silver dust, the dwarves continued their march. Just before arriving at the second passage, another patrol approached them. The dwarves stopped and hid, but the two

Panwolves sensed something and moved right in their direction. They were very close to Radu and Vale, but the goblins pulled them away because they couldn't see anything in that area.

Soon after, when they reached the entrance of the second passage, just before it became visible again, Nikos opened it quickly, and they ran inside, heading directly to the secret part of the lake where the little boat was hidden.

When there, Nikos boarded the boat and began rowing, looking for the moving island to meet with Fedora. He rowed for a few minutes until he encountered a cloud of fog moving in his direction, which covered the boat in seconds. Since he couldn't see where he was going, he stopped rowing, and moments later, he landed on the small island. As he had done before, he exited the boat, sent the magic shell announcing his arrival, and walked to the tree to wait for Fedora.

As she had done before, Fedora emerged from the waters in her majestic way. Nikos greeted her, and the queen returned the greeting and said, "The chosen one has done well, rescuing Henrietta and keeping the ring far from Zoltar's hands. He must be a brave human boy. But now, difficult tasks are ahead, my old friend!"

They moved closer to the small tree, and Fedora made a pair of chairs appear by swinging her Scepter. They sat there, and for the next hour, Nikos told her everything about Andy's visit since his arrival, the liberation of Henrietta, and their safe return to the village. Then Nikos added,

"Fedora, this boy is now waiting for us to tell him what to do next…"

"The Oracle has spoken and told me the following. The lad will need to find the eye of the seeker. Then we'll know how to defeat Zoltar!"

"What is the eye of the seeker?" Nikos asked

"I thought it was a legend, but according to the Oracle, it is pretty much real. The legend said that many centuries ago, during the last war between the kingdoms, Julius, the master sorcerer, had a beautiful sapphire called the Eye of the Seeker, which had the power to reveal what the holder was looking for, what they most wanted, and where to find it. When Julius knew both kings were after the stone, he hid it. He didn't want any of them to have it and used it to their advantage. Legend says that the stone is in a place protected by a monster, and the location of that place is in a clue, which he hid somewhere in the lake."

"But where in the lake can you look for that clue?" Nikos asked her.

"The Oracle said, don't look deep, look wise, and let the ones who sing… tell you the way."

"What's the meaning of that, Fedora?" A confused Nikos asked.

"My friend, the oracle is referring to us, the mermaids. We're the ones who always sing, so the answer must be in one of our old songs. Wait a minute… Why didn't I think of this before? Julius wrote a poem for my daughter Marily when she was born, and she used to recite it when she was little. That's the clue. Bring the lad by the next full moon; we'll be ready. Be careful, though; the forest is full of patrols. Move your village as frequently as possible. If necessary, relocate it near the sea. Zoltar won't suspect you are there!"

"Thank you, Fedora. We'll be careful, and I'll bring the boy personally on the next full moon. I'll send the messengers to give him the news!"

"Now I have to go and start working on finding that clue… good luck, and see you soon, my friend," Fedora said and got in her chariot, returning to the bottom of the lake. Nikos got on the boat, and as it had done before, the boat rowed him back to shore. It was still daylight when he arrived, so he and his escort waited until dark to return to their village.

Later that night, upon arriving at the village, Nikos moved it out of the Emerald Forest for the first time in centuries. Following Fedora's advice, he moved it close to the sea; that was the safest place for them… at least for the time being… and they would have to stay there until Andy completed his next task.

After finishing moving the village, Nikos called Thaddeus and Luscious and said,

"Brothers, you have to go back to the real world and tell Sir Andy he will come for the next task on the next full moon. It'll be a difficult task. All I know for now is that he must be in good shape, and maybe some swimming will be necessary. I'll give you more information as soon as I receive it from Fedora."

The two loyal dwarves immediately started preparations for their journey back to the real world and were excited to see their young master again.

******

More than one month had passed since Andy visited the magical world of Ethernia, and there was no word yet on when he would have to return. He wondered if anything terrible had happened because he hadn't seen his two little friends ever since. Danny and Lucy had been asking him about them almost daily, making Andy's wait even more anxious.

That afternoon, when he got home from school, he wasn't feeling well and did something unusual for him. He passed through the kitchen without opening the fridge and looked for something to eat. Mrs. Muller stared at him, stunned, as he told her, "Hello Helga… I'll be in my room."

When he opened the door to his room, his mood changed completely. Seated on his bed were his two friends, Luscious and Thaddeus. He closed the door and ran to hug them, saying, "Guys! I'm so happy to see you! Where the hell have you been all this time? When will I go back?"

"Easy, Master. We're glad to see you too… We finally have a message for you… from Lord Nikos!"

"Great! Don't make me wait, guys?!"

"You'll go back on the next full moon; there's a new task for you, Master!"

"Cool! What is it?"

"We don't know that yet; Lord Nikos simply said you have to go… and he asked us to prepare you. By the way, Master, do you know how to swim?"

"Of course, I can swim! You forgot that I'm on the swimming team at my school!"

"Good… because he told us that you must be in good shape for the next task, which may include some swimming."

"I haven't swum since summer, but I'm ready. Wait till Danny and Lucy find out that you're here. They had been asking for you two almost daily these last two weeks."

"Well, Master, we only have a little over two weeks until the next full moon… so, starting tomorrow, you'll begin your training!"

They continued to talk and laugh. Andy hadn't looked so happy since he returned from his first trip to Ethernia. His eyes were glowing, and he wasn't thinking about how difficult or dangerous the next task could be. All he cared about was that he would go back to another fantastic and magical adventure in Ethernia…

Chapter Nineteen:" The Second Task

That night after dinner, Andy called Danny to tell him the news. Danny yelled so loud that his mother got scared and opened the door of his room to ask him what was going on. He answered, "Nothing, Mom. It's just that we're having a math test tomorrow!"

"I never saw you that excited about any test before, especially math."

"Come on, Mom, I'm trying to help Andy with this test."

"Okay, son… but your father will never believe this," his mother said as she closed the door.

Andy, who heard that comment, said to Danny, "You liar. When have you been able to help me with any tests? It's always the other way around!"

"I had to get rid of her, okay? Well, I'll see you tomorrow, dude. I'll go to your house after school."

"All right, see you tomorrow," Andy said and hung up the phone.

Lucy came home that night, unaware of the news. As she passed her brother's room, she heard Andy talking to someone. Without blinking, she opened the door and said, "Are they back?"

Andy only pointed at the two little men standing by his bed, and before she could say anything else, the dwarves told her, "Good to see you again, Lady Lucy."

She closed the door and responded, "It's Good to see you guys. We were wondering when you would show up again."

During the next two weeks, Andy spent most of his free time training. His parents wondered why he had developed a sudden interest in exercising in the middle of winter. Meanwhile, Lucy had been studying for her mid-term exams, but something unusual had bothered her since the dwarves returned. Her birthmark, in the shape of a rose, had been itching on and off, and she didn't know why.

But two nights before the beginning of the full moon, Lucy had a weird dream and decided finally to ask the dwarves if there was any connection between that and the itching. The next day, after her last midterm exam, she returned home and went directly to Andy's room. When inside and before she could say anything, Thaddeus asked her, "Lady Lucy, what's bothering you? You look a little distressed… did everything go okay with the exams?"

"Hello Thaddeus, the exams were fine… but there's something else."

Thaddeus said, "My lady, what is it? Please tell us."

She showed him her birthmark and said, "This area on my arm has been itching since you returned, and last night, I had a weird dream. I saw Andy swimming through a waterfall. The current was pulling him in, but he was swimming harder. I saw a dagger in one of his hands. Then, just before he was about to pass through the waterfall, a mermaid came and grabbed him. After that, everything went blurry. Then, all I could hear was a huge roar… and I woke up."

"Well, Lady Lucy, I think there's a connection; your dreams are giving you a vision of what may happen in the future, and the itching was the message announcing that dream. Now I understand why Nikos told me to ensure that Master Andy knows how to swim. So, the visions in your dreams could be part of the next task!"

******

At Crystal Lake, Fedora and the mermaids were still working to solve the clue in Marily's poem. It was called "the blue star" and was given to her by Julius, the Master Sorcerer. In one of the verses lies the clue to find the Eye of the Seeker.

They read the poem repeatedly until Marily realized the middle verse was the clue. Her mother noticed, too, and said, "Repeat that verse, Marily. I think that's the clue!"

"When the sun appears after the rain, and the rainbow touches the lake."

"Through the color of your eyes, find the way to the blue star."

"When you find a water wall, don't think you got it wrong."

"Sing, and he will go to sleep; get the star, and the truth will set you free."

"That's it… that's the clue! Let's find out what it means, girls!" the queen told the other mermaids. "We have a couple of days before the human lad comes!"

They were determined to find the answer before Andy's arrival.

******

The first day of the full moon finally arrived, and with that, the next trip to Ethernia. Andy spent most of the day with Danny at the mall, trying to stay distracted and avoid thinking about his next task.

Because his parents went out with some friends, Andy and the dwarves had to wait until they returned before going to the attic. Thus, when they finished supper, Andy and Danny played video games to kill some time. The two dwarves watched, stunned by how skillful the two youths were with what they called the magical box. Lucy went out with her friends but came back early.

At around eleven thirty, Andy's parents came home from their dinner. Before going to bed, they went to check on Andy and Danny. The boys were in their pajamas, still playing, when Conrad opened the door and said,

"Good night, boys. Don't stay up too late, okay."

"Good night, boys," Helen said in the background.

"Okay, Dad…Good night. Good night, Mom!" Andy replied, and Danny added, "Good night, Mr. and Mrs. Logan."

As soon as Andy's parents had gone to their room, Luscious put them to sleep as he had done before.

Andy changed into his Ethernia clothes, which had been hidden in his closet since the last time, and went to fetch the keys to the attic with Danny. Minutes later, Lucy and the dwarves joined them in the attic. Since they were familiar with the routine, they proceeded directly to business. They removed the music box from the chest and placed it on the table, then moved the table to the center of the room, where the moonlight would hit it directly. They opened the music box, and the green cloud appeared on the table when the moonlight touched it.

The same letters as before were taking shape on top of that music box, and Andy, holding the golden key, yelled: AURA GATE ... AURA GATE!!!

Everyone expected the floor to open and let the door emerge as it had the first time. But this time, it was different. The ceiling rumbled and opened up, allowing the beautiful golden door to come crashing down. Everyone was utterly astonished at how the beautiful door had reappeared so magically.

"Wow! Did you see that?!" Danny yelled. And then Andy said,

"This time, it came from the ceiling; why Thaddeus?"

"Master, the gate decided where to come from. I don't know exactly why. We must go now. Have the key ready to open the door!"

Andy turned to Lucy and hugged her, telling her, "Goodbye, Sis, thank you for being here. See you soon!"

"Shut up, Andy; I wanted to be here. Goodbye, and good luck. Don't forget, I want a full description!"

Danny hugged him, too, and said, "Goodbye, dude. Good luck and bring me a souvenir... Just kidding!"

Then Andy pulled the key out of his pocket and unlocked the door. The emerald in the center opened up like a mouth and told him,

"WELCOME BACK, MASTER,..."

The door opened, revealing the multicolored portal that covered the tunnel. Andy and the dwarves disappeared through it, and the door closed. Seconds later, a tiny voice called Lucy again, saying, "Greetings, Lady Lucy and Sir Danny, it's good to see you again and so soon!"

"Oh, it's nice to see you too, but it has been almost two months since our last time here. We didn't know if we'd see you tonight either," Lucy said.

"What do you mean, two months!? It seemed like we were here with you only moments ago… and where's Sir Andy?"

"My brother just went back to Ethernia to meet the second task. By opening the golden door, your enchantment weakened, and you came alive again, but the effects will end at sunrise."

"I understand… so, we're back, but only until morning."

"Yes, I'm afraid so," Lucy told them.

Lucy grabbed her hands and asked them to tell their own story of how they had met at the lake and fallen in love; Nolan and Morgana looked at each other and chuckled, and then the princess started to tell their story.

******

Andy and his friends were reaching the end of the tunnel and getting ready to jump. There wouldn't be any mistakes this time, as Andy knew exactly what to do.

Seconds later, they were walking in an area of the forest closer to the ocean. This area was almost untouched by all the plagues Zoltar sent over the years. They got to the small labyrinth that took them to the dwarf village. They arrived almost at dawn, and a welcome committee was awaiting them. Following the greetings, they were escorted to Nikos' cabin. The chief of the dwarves opened his arms and said to Andy, "Welcome back, Sir Andy! It's a joy to see you again!"

"Great to see you too, Lord Nikos. Tell me, what do I have to do now?"

"We shall depart for Crystal Lake right after breakfast. We must get there before dark. Fedora will inform us of the next steps. So, enjoy a cup of hot chocolate and tell me how your journey was this time.

"Quieter! I knew how to get out of the tunnel this time, and the labyrinth part was faster; why, Lord Nikos?"

"Because the labyrinth brought you out of the forest, closer to the ocean. We are far from the cities, and the passages are shorter."

Then Nikos gave him a cup of hot chocolate and sent him to rest in the cabin, which had been prepared for him. So, after a couple of hours, Lumi woke Andy up and took him to the main cabin, where her father and the others were waiting for him.

During breakfast, Andy had the opportunity to greet Lady Henrietta, who warmly hugged him and wished him the best of luck in his new task. Andy told her about Nolan and Morgana and how they had come back to life momentarily during his time in Ethernia. This news made Henrietta give a big sigh of relief. Then, Nikos provided the details about their journey to the lake. They would take the silver dust, but it may not be enough to cover the time needed to cross the area he chose to get from one passage to the other, so we'll use it when necessary. The selected area was the most treacherous part of the forest, teeming with wild creatures, including giant bats and Panwolves. However, it was an area with fewer chances of encountering a patrol. For protection, Nikos ordered a special potion to block the Panwolves' heightened sense of smell and instructed the group to exercise extreme caution. The same dwarves chosen for the first mission were selected again: Luscious, Thaddeus, Radu, Vale, and Kaleb.

When breakfast ended, Nikos, Andy, and their escort left the main cottage, heading to the secret passage, which was located at the south end of the village. When they entered, no one spoke so as not to disturb the bushes... they crossed it as fast as they could. When they exited the passage, the area seemed too quiet, and Nikos, an old fox (close to 1000 years in age), told them, "Sir Andy and brothers... be careful! Have your silver dust ready!"

Radu was at the front, with Kaleb and the rest a few yards behind. Suddenly, Radu spotted a large patrol approaching. He turned quickly, and as he was sending the signal to the others, a giant bat attacked him out of nowhere. Kaleb came to help, hitting the beast on the head (its weak point) and making the monster fly away. Radu was severely injured, and the patrol was coming his way, so Kaleb hid him quickly under some bushes.

About two hundred feet behind, Andy and the others heard the signal and hid just in time, barely missing the patrol and, thanks to the special potion, avoided being smelled by the Panwolves. They approached Kaleb and Radu, and Nikos immediately tended to the injured dwarf; then, he said,

"We'll have to carry him. We can't cure him now; the patrol may return soon. Let's go. Everyone… use the dust now!"

"Nikos, let me carry him! It'll be faster this way!" Andy replied.

A grateful Nikos responded, "You're truly the chosen one, Sir Andy." Everyone used the dust, including Radu, and continued their march to reach the second passage, through one of the darkest areas of the forest.

When they arrived at the entrance to the passage, the effects of the dust were gone, and they were all visible again. Nikos asked Andy to put Radu down so he could tend to his injuries, and Andy could rest. Radu was unconscious and very pale. Nikos tended to him immediately, but Radu wasn't responding; he had lost too much blood and was dying. Everyone looked at him in silence, watching how Nikos was doing everything he could to save their friend, until the dwarf lord stood up and turned to the others,

"Our brother Radu, the warrior, has just crossed the river of death…" All the dwarves removed their hats and lowered their heads. A profound silence followed Nikos' words, and Andy even shed a tear. Their first casualty had just happened…something the human lad wasn't prepared for.

Chapter Twenty: The Stone's Guardian

They opened the second passage and took Radu's body to be buried by the lake. While going through the passage, no one said a word; you could see everyone's sadness on their faces; their mood differed from the one in the first labyrinth. When they reached the end, Nikos opened the wall, and there was the secret part of the lake where Fedora's little boat was hiding.

After a short but emotional funeral, they buried Radu by the closest willow tree. Then, without any time to mourn, Nikos and Andy quickly jumped into the little boat and started rowing until they found the fog, which immediately surrounded them. Moments later, they landed on the little island, and Nikos told Andy, "Let me send the magic shell to announce to Fedora that we are here." Then, he added, "Let's go by the tree and wait there. The Queen will be here hopefully soon."

They sat there for about an hour and didn't talk much. The loss of Radu was too painful for Nikos, and Andy was still impressed by that. Their silence was suddenly interrupted by a huge splash from the lake. The magnificent shell chariot came out of the waters, bringing Fedora, the good queen of the Lake, and her daughter Marily. In her powerful voice, the queen said, "Greetings, Nikos… and you must be the human lad, Andy… Greetings to you, too, and welcome to my kingdom!"

Andy was stunned by the scene and the beauty of the young mermaid. He stared at her, utterly speechless… and they exchanged smiles without saying a word. Nikos broke the silence: "Your Majesty, allow me to present you, Sir Andy Logan, the Keymaster!"

As the chariot landed on the little island, something unique happened in front of Andy and Nikos. The mermaids' fins were transformed into human legs in seconds. Andy couldn't believe what he saw; he stood there wholly flabbergasted… When he snapped out of it, he almost stuttered, "Yo… your Ma… ajesty, it's an honor to meet you!"

Andy bowed to her and once again exchanged looks with Marily. Then, the Queen introduced her daughter to Andy. "Young sir, this is my daughter, Princess Marily of Crystal Lake!"

"Princess Marily, it's a pleasure to make your acquaintance!" a bashful Andy responded.

"Thank you, young sir; the pleasure is mine!" Marily responded.

Marily looked like a teenage human girl, probably around sixteen years old, and was stunningly beautiful with her long brown hair and striking green eyes. Andy was quite impressed and couldn't take his eyes off her; she seemed to feel the same attraction, as evidenced by the way she exchanged looks with him. Then, the queen stated,

"We found the clue! Julius wrote it in the poem for Marily when she was born. We need to follow the rainbow and look through the green color to find the way to the blue star (the sapphire, also known as the eye of the seeker). All we have to do is follow the directions, but we must be careful. A monster is protecting the stone…and you, young sir, will have to fight with him."

"But, Fedora, we are in a dry season, and to have a rainbow, we need rain first, and Andy can stay only four more days!" Nikos interrupted.

"The Oracle has announced a rainfall for tomorrow morning. You two will spend the night here; we'll return after the rain tomorrow." Then, she made a nice tent appear in the middle of that little island by swinging her Scepter. After a short goodbye, the mermaids returned to the water, but not before Marily and Andy exchanged another tender look.

Andy was so fascinated with the mermaids that he spent the rest of the night asking Nikos several questions about them. Andy was particularly interested in how these beautiful creatures got their human legs when they touched dry land.

"All mermaids can transform themselves into humans on dry land, but only for a few days each time. If they stay more than seven days, they become humans permanently, losing all their powers as mermaids. Did you know that they can live more than two thousand years? Fedora is about twelve hundred years old and looks like a human woman in her forties, and Marily is about eight hundred and looks like a human teenager!" Nikos said.

"How is that possible, Lord Nikos?"

"Because in the water, time passes very slowly, and they age at a different pace… compared to your world."

"Wow, that's amazing! I can't believe all the things I have seen so far! Sometimes I wonder… if everything is real or… I'm dreaming…"

"Maybe it's a dream, after all. We'll see how it ends. Now, let's rest; tomorrow will be a busy day!" Nikos finally said.

So, they went to sleep, but Andy still had many questions in his mind. He would have to find the answers as they were presented during the next few days.

The next morning, they were awakened by a beautiful melody. Andy came out quickly and found three beautiful mermaids humming that captivating melody. When the mermaids saw him, they chorused, "Good morning, young sir! Welcome to Crystal Lake!" They looked at each other and giggled.

"Good morning, ladies! My name is Andy Logan, and it's a pleasure to meet you."

"We are Rosi, Lori, and Alexia, best friends of Princess Marily. It's our pleasure to make your acquaintance. We're here to tell you that it'll rain soon, and you must be prepared."

"Thank you, ladies, we'll be ready!"

Seconds later, Nikos came out of the tent. As he greeted the mermaids, a dark cloud covered that part of the lake, followed by the first thunder roaring, announcing the upcoming rain. The three mermaids went back to the bottom of the lake as Andy and Nikos got back inside the tent. It rained heavily for almost an hour, accompanied by strong winds and thunder, but Andy and Nikos were well protected inside the tent, thanks to the magic of Fedora.

When the rain stopped, they emerged from the tent. The sky was clear, and they could see one of the biggest and most beautiful rainbows anyone had ever seen.

A big splash was heard, and the magnificent shell chariot came from the water, carrying Fedora and Marily.

"Good day, Nikos and young Sir. Please get in the boat; don't touch the oars; they will row magically and follow me; we have to get to the end of the rainbow before it disappears!" the queen said.

They followed the queen for a few minutes, and Andy was thinking: *How can we get to the rainbow? It's an optical illusion, and no one can touch it...!*

But Andy forgot that he was in Ethernia, where everything is possible!

As they approached one of the rainbow's ends, Andy couldn't believe that he was seeing the actual end of a rainbow. When they finally arrived, the Queen told her daughter to go and see through the green color. Marily quickly swam to the rainbow, and when she got there and looked, she exclaimed, "Mother, I see a waterfall. It seems like the one in the Diamond River, but it looks a little fuzzy!"

Suddenly, Andy took the cape and shoes off, jumped into the water, and swam to where Marily was. Then he touched the green color of the rainbow with the ring of clovers. A magnified vision appeared, showing the way to the waterfall. Everyone there looked a little confused and surprised. Andy turned to Marily, and for a moment, they exchanged such a tender look that some attraction had blossomed between them.

Then Fedora spoke in a commanding voice,

"Nikos, I'll take you back to shore. You, young sir, will follow my daughter in the small boat. I will send three mermaids to help you. Remember this: When you get to the waterfall, you must swim through it to find the blue sapphire. There is a monster protecting the stone. I can't use my magic on that monster, so the mermaids will sing to put him to sleep.

Then, you'll have to take the stone. Be ready to use your dagger if necessary. We'll be waiting for you!"

"My dagger… why, Your Majesty?"

"The truth will set you free. That's what the clue said, young sir, and that's the dagger of truth. Now go… and good luck!"

Before leaving, Andy gave his clothes to Nikos and stayed in his swimwear. Then Fedora pointed her wand at the boat, and the oars started rowing fast, enabling Andy to follow Marily, who was swimming faster in the direction of the merging point of the diamond river with the lake. The princess stopped and told Andy, "Young Sir, we'll go slower from here. The waterfall is about three miles upriver, and I will swim by your side. Be ready to jump out of the boat when I tell you!"

"Please call me Andy. If we're going to do this together, I want us to be friends, okay, Marily?"

"Okay, Andy." They smiled at each other. Then Andy winked at her and said, "I don't know if anybody told you this before, but you are gorgeous!"

"Awwww… Thank you… So are you!" she responded. Andy was a handsome young man, almost 6 feet tall, with brown hair and hazel eyes. He opened his eyes in surprise when he heard what the mermaid said and started thinking, *this is like a dream! I am here in this fantastic land, talking with the most beautiful girl that I've ever seen, and this girl is a mermaid!* Then he said, "You're the first mermaid I've ever seen!"

"Oh, please, Andy, don't embarrass me. Don't tell me that you've never seen a mermaid before?!"

"Of course not; in my world, mermaids are mythical creatures; no one has seen one… ever!"

At that precise moment, the three mermaids sent by Fedora appeared right behind them and sang at once:

"Greetings, Marily, and young sir… We're here to help you!"

"Shhh… don't be so loud!" Marily whispered. "We don't know what kinds of creatures are in these waters!"

The three mermaids nodded and stayed silent for the rest of the way. However, Marily and Andy kept exchanging looks, and the other mermaids chuckled and whispered in the back each time the human boy and the mermaid princess looked at each other.

When they got closer to the waterfall, Marily told Andy, "We must leave the boat here; the current will break it. You'll have to swim from here."

So, Andy rowed to shore and, after securing the boat, went back to the river. He was swimming along with the mermaids, and as they were getting closer to the waterfall, it was harder for Andy to swim. The current was strong on the surface. Then Marily said, "We'll have to go underwater now. You'll have to hold your breath as long as you can. Get ready!"

"Okay!" Andy yelled.

Andy and the four mermaids went underwater and began swimming across the waterfall. The mermaids quickly went through, but Andy was struggling. Time passed, and the mermaids were waiting for him on the other side. He was swimming harder but getting weaker and almost out of air in his lungs. When Marily saw him, she immediately went back to help him. She grabbed his hands and kissed him on the mouth, giving him the necessary energy to continue. He felt his lungs fill with air and started to swim faster to cross to the other side of the falls. Amazingly, it was completely calm on the other side, so they went up to the surface. Then, Marily asked Andy, "Are you okay?"

Andy, staring at her eyes and still panting, said, "Thank you, Marily, you saved my life!"

They grabbed their hands for a second and continued swimming inside the cave, searching for the blue stone. Finally, they arrived at a small tunnel, which led them to a small pond located inside a large cave. Daylight streamed through a hole in the ceiling, revealing the blue and clear water in the pond. They all looked around until Andy spotted the bright blue sapphire lying on top of a rock in the shape of a crab. Then, pointing at it, he yelled, "Over there! On that rock... that must be the eye of the seeker." Marily signaled him to lower his voice, but it was too late; a colossal roar was heard, making the cave rumble, and its echo was so loud that Andy and the mermaids had to cover their ears.

To everyone's horror, a gigantic crab came from one of the caves, snapping its pincers. Marily quickly grabbed Andy and submerged him in the water while the other three mermaids started to sing a very soft melody, causing the monster to calm down and fall asleep.

When the monster fell asleep, the mermaids signaled Andy and Marily to proceed, so they quickly got out of the water. Once again, Andy looked in awe at how Marily's fins transformed into human legs. They moved carefully, walking towards the rock where the Sapphire was resting. They could hear the mermaids singing and the monster snoring. Andy was holding Marily's hand the entire time. Then she told him, "Andy, be careful. There must be some traps. I don't think it'll be that easy to pull the stone from there!"

"You might be right, Marily. We must be ready to return to the water as soon as I grab the stone…"

When they got in front of the stone, they stared at it with their eyes wide open. It was a big and beautiful sapphire, about the size of an adult fist, perfectly cut. Just before pulling the sapphire, Andy looked around again, noticing many bones and skulls on the other side of the rock! Then, he knew that others had come before, but couldn't get the stone. He kept looking around for possible traps, finding many tiny round holes in the wall behind the rock. Thinking for a moment, he remembered one of the *Indiana Jones* movies he liked so much, and showing the holes to Marily, he whispered, "Look, that's the trap. We have to pull the sapphire and duck immediately. Those holes will shoot something at us as soon as I pull on the stone." He also showed her the bones behind the rock. She freaked out at the sight but managed to hold in the scream.

He asked Marily to bend down as he was ready to grab the sapphire. Suddenly, the walls began to crack, waking up the monster. Andy quickly grabbed the stone with one hand and pulled Marily even lower, ducking himself at the same time as poisoned darts shot out from the round holes and passed over their heads. Then he yelled, "We have to get to the water!"

They jumped from the rocks, avoiding the darts, but the monster was fully awake and came right at them, pointing its pincers. Marily yelled, "Get your dagger out… now!"

Andy gave the sapphire to Marily and pulled his dagger out, yelling at her, "Jump in the water, now! I'll try to distract him… My God, he's so huge! Where do I hit him?"

"The eyes! The eyes!" The mermaids yelled, and when Marily was ready to jump into the water, the monster caught her with one of his pincers just as Andy was avoiding the other pincer. She yelled out of pain. That was all Andy needed to draw strength and attack the monster. He got a little closer… He knew he would have only one shot.

"The truth will set me free!" he yelled, aiming at one of the monster's eyes; he threw his dagger at the target.

The monster immediately released the girl and began to struggle for his life. Andy came to help Marily, who was wounded and unconscious. Almost at the same time, the three mermaids yelled at him, "Take her to the water… now!"

Andy grabbed Marily and the stone and carried her to the water without a moment to lose. There, he was in awe of how she was turning back into a mermaid and how her wounds were healing. When she awoke, Andy hugged her and said, "Thank God you're okay!"

A loud tremor was heard, and the cave started falling apart, so Andy yelled, "We've got to get out of here now!" And everyone quickly began swimming out of the pond. Andy was holding the stone and couldn't swim well, so Marily and Lori grabbed him and submerged him underwater. Marily gave him another kiss on the mouth right before the surprised Lori. Then, they started swimming faster, crossing the tunnels back to the waterfall in seconds, while the cave collapsed and many rocks fell into the water.

When they finally reached the boat, Andy's first reaction was to pull Marily closer. Before she could say anything, he kissed her tenderly on the mouth. The other three mermaids watched, utterly stunned by how the human boy kissed their princess.

After the kiss, Andy said, "We did it… we did it, thank you! We have the eye of the seeker!"

"Yes, Andy, we did it, but we must leave this place right now…"

A huge rumble was heard coming from behind the waterfall. Andy and the mermaids looked at each other, and like a stroke of lightning, Andy pushed the boat back into the water, and the four mermaids began pushing it out of the area as fast as they could. Suddenly, a huge wave came out of the waterfall, coming in their direction. They tried to get back into the lake before the wave broke, but it was going so fast that it broke down only a few yards before reaching the lake; flipping the boat over, all Andy could do was secure the stone in his hands, but the wave submerged him deep into the water.

The mermaids immediately helped him to the surface. The current was so strong that without their help, he would have drowned. At the surface, they turned the boat and helped Andy to get there, after which they continued with their journey back to the place where Fedora, Nikos, and the other dwarves were waiting for them.

On their way to meet Fedora and Nikos, Andy asked Marily if she could join him in the boat. She hesitated for a moment but then accepted. He helped her get in, but her fins didn't change this time. The two oars were rowing by themselves, and they were looking at each other so tenderly that Andy could not resist and kissed her again. The other mermaids laughed and whispered, making the two young lovers blush. Then, Marily started to hum a beautiful melody that put Andy to sleep in no time. She kissed him and told the others, "He needs the rest." So, after laying him down in the boat, she jumped back into the water.

Andy was sleeping, and one could see the brightness of satisfaction on his face. The second challenge had been accomplished, and now the queen was waiting for him; together, they were about to discover the one true thing that could destroy the evil Zoltar.

Chapter Twenty-one: The Scepter of Julius

Andy slept for almost an hour, and when he awoke, he found himself alone in the boat with the oars not moving; none of the mermaids were around, so he began to call Marily.

"Marily!? Marily!? Where are you?" But he got no answer. By then, the sun was beginning to set on the horizon, and he was getting closer to the north shore of the lake, where Fedora and the dwarves were waiting for him. Then, he began to row in that direction when a familiar voice said, "Hello, Andy! Did you sleep well?"

He stopped rowing, and there she was, Marily, smiling at him with her arms resting on the edge of the boat.

"Oh, I'm glad to see you. You got me quite scared. I thought something had happened to you and the others!"

"We left to let you rest and refresh ourselves. My mother and the dwarves are waiting for us; we are getting closer."

As they approached shore, Andy got a good view of Fedora and the dwarves. He stood up in the boat, and after waving at them, he raised his hand, showing them the gorgeous sapphire. The queen and Nikos returned big smiles of satisfaction.

When the boat landed, Nikos and the other dwarves surrounded Andy, embraced him, and began yelling, "Bravo, sir Andy, well done!" Then, approaching the queen, he bowed and gave her the eye of the seeker. The queen took it and said,

"Well done, young sir! Superb work; you've brought us the blue sapphire, also known as the eye of the seeker! Bravo!"

"Your Majesty, without Princess Marily and the mermaids, I couldn't have done it. They deserve even more credit than I do!"

"Young sir, it's very kind of you to recognize the effort of others. You're indeed well educated. The most important thing is knowing how to use this stone. I'll ask my oracle and-"

Before she could finish that sentence, Andy's left arm began shaking fast. He tried to hold it with his right hand, but it was too strong for him. Suddenly, a blue light came out of the ring. So, he yelled, "I can't stop it! I think the ring is trying to tell me something!"

Nikos noticed and yelled, "Fedora, give Andy back the eye of the seeker. I think that's what the ring wants!"

Fedora gave the stone back to Andy, and almost immediately, his left arm stopped shaking, but the ring's blue light was still on. Andy then knew it was time to pull out the ring from his finger and see if there was a new message. He gave the stone momentarily to the queen, but he asked her to stay closer to him. When he pulled the ring off his finger, the light disappeared, and he could see a new inscription.

"What can destroy the devil's heart?"

After a long pause, Nikos said, "That's a question; that is what you have to ask the stone, Andy. The sapphire will tell you what can destroy Zoltar's heart and where to find it!"

Andy put the ring back on his finger, and the queen gave him the stone again, saying, "Go ahead, young sir, ask the stone what you want to know."

He grabbed the stone with both hands and asked, "Show me what can destroy the devil's heart!"

A bright light surrounded the stone, and an object appeared inside. Andy's hands trembled, and everyone around him looked with their eyes wide open.

The image became clearer, revealing a beautiful golden Scepter. The queen, almost yelling, said, "That Scepter looks familiar to me. It's almost like mine but with a ruby in the middle. I think I know! That's the Scepter of Julius, the master sorcerer! Zoltar was his protégé. So, it makes sense that the only weapon that can destroy him is that. We need to search for it as soon as we can. Sir Andy, ask the stone where we can find the Scepter of Julius!"

Andy immediately brought the stone closer to his face and asked, "Where can I find the Scepter of Julius?"

The bright light appeared again, followed by a new apparition. This time, it was the summit of an icy mountain. Then Nikos exclaimed, "That's the frozen mountain, one of the highest and coldest on the north side of the forbidden mountains!"

"You're right, Nikos; we need to get that Scepter, but it will take some time... so we must prepare everything for it. We'll have to do it during the next full moon. Now I'll return to the lake, taking the stone with me; it'll be safer there. I'll consult the oracle for any future advice. Nikos, you and Andy need to be back in the village before sunrise so he can return home safely. Once again, well done, Andy! You're indeed a brave and clever lad! Let's enjoy some food and drinks before you go."

At that moment, Fedora swung her Scepter, and a long table full of food and beverages appeared for everyone's enjoyment.

For the next hour, everyone enjoyed the feast, including Andy, who, after the effort of the last task, was so hungry that they could eat a whole chicken. Andy spent most of the time close to Marily. The queen was so occupied making plans with Nikos that she didn't observe the apparent attraction between her daughter and the human lad. When Fedora finished with Nikos, she called her daughter, saying. "Marily, it's time to go. These people have to go back to their village."

"Yes, Mother. Give me a moment!" Then she said goodbye to Andy, kissing him on the cheek, while the mother lifted her eyebrows in surprise.

Right after that, the shell's chariot came out of the water; Fedora and Marily got on it and waved goodbye to Andy and the dwarves, returning to the bottom of the lake. Seconds later, the table and the remaining goodies vanished, leaving the area as it had been before the feast.

Andy and the dwarves began their journey back to the village. They wanted to get there before dawn, so they crossed the first passage quickly. When they arrived at the area between passages, one of the darkest parts of the forest, they were forced to slow their pace due to the dense foliage and the uneven ground.

When they finally arrived at the second passage, they found a small patrol of two goblins, two trolls, and a Panwolf resting close to the entrance (Without the patrol knowing). They had to pass through them to get to the labyrinth. Nikos knew using the silver dust wouldn't be enough since the Panwolf could detect them with his highly sensitive sense of smell. They needed to drug the Panwolf first, but one had to get close to the beast for a clear shot.

Vale volunteered for the task, but he only had two darts left, and it wouldn't be enough for all the goblins if they woke up. Nikos agreed but ordered the other dwarves and Andy to be ready to fight if the goblins woke up. Vale was practically slithering to get closer to the Panwolf, which began to feel his presence. Then, the Panwolf stood up and roared right when Vale shot at him with one of his darts.

The Panwolf collapsed right there, but the noise awoke one of the goblins, who immediately awoke the other guards. Andy, remembering his magic shoes, began to run around the guards. After grabbing one of their clubs, he quickly knocked down the two trolls and one of the goblins. But the last goblin desperately swung his club, hitting Andy on the head and knocking him down. When the goblin was about to hit the unconscious Andy again, Vale shot him with his last dart, putting him to sleep instantly.

Moments later, Andy awoke but was a little dizzy, and Nikos ordered everyone to move quickly to the entrance before the goblins regained consciousness. Luscious and Thaddeus had to help Andy. Then, Nikos, waving his right hand, said, *"Lasamikus in,"* and the passage opened.

They entered the labyrinth, and one of the goblins opened his eyes and saw the wall closing behind Andy and the dwarves. "Ohh," he mumbled… and then thought, *a secret passage; Lord Zoltar needs to know this… I'll be rewarded.*

Andy and the dwarves arrived at the village by the crack of dawn. Andy was still a little dizzy, with a bump on his head. He was taken directly to Nikos' cabin, where he was cured with special herbs. He rested for a couple of hours and awoke feeling better (the bump on his head was gone, and the last thing he remembered was when they were about to attack the goblins). He asked Thaddeus, "What happened? I can't remember anything after we attacked those goblins! I don't even remember the labyrinth!"

"Don't trouble yourself, master; it was the medicine we used to cure you. One of the goblins hit you with his club, and you were unconscious for a while. Now you're fine and ready to go back home!"

"Thanks, Thaddeus. I feel better now; what do we do next?"

"You have to go home now, Master. The Golden Gate only opens during the full moon, and we only have one more day. We'll prepare everything for your next task: finding the Scepter of Julius. As soon as we know the details, Luscious and I will go to see you."

"I should miss you all, especially Marily; I can't get her out of my mind!"

"Master, remember that she's a mermaid, and you're a human!"

"I know… but I never felt this way before!" Andy replied, while Thaddeus only nodded.

After a brief goodbye, Andy left, accompanied only by Luscious and Thaddeus. Nikos and the entire dwarf nation were preparing to mourn the loss of Radu, and nobody from the village would walk with them to the passage.

Thaddeus opened the passage, and the three of them entered in silence. Andy was thinking about all his new experiences during this visit to Ethernia, and he could hardly wait to get back to the attic and tell Danny and Lucy about them.

What he and the dwarves couldn't imagine was that by then, Zoltar had received the report from the goblins about the dwarves' secret passages in the forest, which would bring the Evil Lord's rage to the Dwarf people.

Chapter Twenty-two: Closing the Labyrinths

Andy and his two little friends arrived at the place where he had to call for the twister that would take him home. After saying goodbye, Andy raised his hand and, grabbing the golden key, yelled the magic words, "AURUS WIND... AURUS WIND... COME TO PICK UP THE GOLDEN KEY!"

The little twister appeared, and Andy jumped in without delay. He was then taken back to the tunnel leading to the gate in his attic.

Meanwhile, in the attic, Lucy and Danny had spent over three hours talking to the prince and princess, and they wondered when Andy would return. They were curious to hear what news he would bring.

Moments later, they heard footsteps, and the oval door opened again, showing the portal. Andy was crossing through it, and he was home again. But this time, something was different. His expression looked more mature. He wasn't smiling but looked more determined. Lucy and Danny immediately got closer and hugged him.

"Andy, there's something different in your expression. What happened this time?" Lucy asked.

"Oh, sis, I have so much to tell you, but first, let me ask you. What about the prince and princess? Are they back?"

"Of course, they're back! Come and see for yourself!"

Andy approached the music box, and the prince and princess greeted him graciously. "We're glad to see you again, young sir. We're eager to hear what you have to tell us."

"Well, I'm glad to see you too, and you're right; there's so much to tell. The most important thing is that now we know how to destroy Zoltar!"

"How is that possible, young sir?" Princess Morgana asked.

"Well, allow me to start from the beginning."

Andy began to tell his story, and everyone in the attic listened attentively. When he got to the part about Radu's death, Lucy and Princess Morgana couldn't hide their emotion and shed a few tears. Andy paused to console the girls and said, "I feel sad, too, but he died saving our lives!"

Then Andy continued with the story. Next, he described his meeting with Fedora, Marily, and the mermaids, and his eyes glowed entirely as he spoke about Marily. Lucy noticed it and began teasing him, "Wow, Andy… mermaids… are they beautiful?"

"Of course, they're beautiful. Shut up, and don't interrupt me, please!" Andy retorted.

Next, Andy told them about the rainbow and how they could touch it and see through it. Lucy and Danny looked like they were listening to a fairy tale, and the princes were remembering how beautiful their magical land was.

When Andy reached the part where he and the mermaids arrived at the waterfall and Marily kissed him underwater to help him swim, he felt embarrassed because the others started laughing. Lucy looked at her brother and saw that expression of tenderness again when he mentioned Marily.

The climax occurs when Andy recounts how he obtained the stone and fought the monster to save Marily. Everyone in the attic was so excited that they began cheering him on.

Finally, Andy mentioned the ring and how it gave him a clue about what to ask the stone to destroy Zoltar; then, the stone shows them the Scepter of Julius.

Nolan looked at Morgana and interrupted Andy, saying, "Julius… Morgana, he was Zoltar's teacher. This makes sense! He taught him everything he knew before Zoltar turned to black magic and killed him!"

By that time, it was almost sunrise. Everyone in the attic was fascinated. Lucy asked her brother, "Andy, what will be next…? What else do you have to do now?"

"All they told me is that I'll go back on the next full moon. Thaddeus and Luscious should be back soon with more details."

Danny was so excited that he looked like a kid receiving his dream Christmas toy. He hugged Andy and told him how proud he was of him. Then Nolan said, "Young sir, we're indeed very grateful for what you are doing to save our land!"

The morning twilight broke through the small window of the attic, and precisely like after Andy's first trip to Ethernia, the prince and princess went to the center of the box. Lucy, who started feeling attached to them, said, "Goodbye, Morgana and Nolan. We'll see you at the next full moon; soon, you shall be free!"

"Goodbye, dear friends. We'll see you again soon!" They answered and immediately turned to their fixed positions. Andy and the others put everything back and went to sleep before somebody noticed they were awake.

******

At Ethernia, Zoltar had been informed about the secret passages the dwarves used to move around the Emerald Forest. He immediately ordered a full search for those passages, as well as looking for anyone who was or had been in contact with the dwarves. The interrogations were merciless, and many people suffered Zoltar's rage.

When the terrible news reached Nikos, he ordered the sealing of all the passages before Zoltar could find them and the dwarf village. He also asked his people to be prepared to defend their Village if necessary. Then, he started preparations for Andy's next visit.

Unfortunately, a few days later, when a group of dwarves finished sealing off the last labyrinth, Morton's soldiers discovered them. The dwarves barely escaped, but the soldiers had enough time to mark the exact location. Thus, after receiving this information, Morton left a group of trolls and goblins guarding the place and went personally to report the news to Zoltar.

When Nikos received the bad news, knowing that Simon could open that passage and trace the path to the village, he took no chances and ordered that all the village entrances be covered up and that he be prepared to fight.

******

It had been over three long weeks since Andy returned from Ethernia, and he hadn't heard from his two small friends yet. The following complete moon phase was only five days away, and he was beginning to get nervous. That night, he was having a nightmare, hearing people crying and yelling for help. So, he awoke very disturbed. Then, he heard the same crying coming out of his closet, where the ring of clovers was hidden. He went on to check the ring and found it emitting a red light. He knew it was another message. He took the ring, returned to bed, and turned the light on. Then, he saw an inscription inside the ring.

Blood is all over the land!

Andy was so preoccupied with this message that he couldn't sleep anymore. He spent the rest of the night wondering what was happening in Ethernia and asked himself *when I would see Luscious and Thaddeus again and find out how to get the Scepter of Julius.*

The following morning at school, Andy told Danny about his dream and the message on the ring, and Danny said, "Something is wrong. What if Zoltar found the dwarf village!"

Andy didn't like Danny's comment and responded, "Shut up. Don't ever say that! You know what could happen if that's true! It'll be the end of the entire dwarf nation!"

"Sorry, dude, but that's the first thing that came to mind!" Danny said

When Andy returned home that afternoon, he found the confirmation of his worries. Luscious and Thaddeus were waiting in his room, but their faces were not smiling this time. Andy immediately asked them, "Guys, I'm glad to see you… Tell me, what's going on?"

"Master, I'm afraid we have bad news. Zoltar's army attacked our Village. Some of our brothers and sisters died in the fight, and many were captured, including some children. Nikos and the rest of us escaped to the caverns by the far side of the mountains, where we could be protected, but not for long. We have until the end of the next full moon to turn ourselves in and pledge loyalty to Zoltar. Otherwise, he will start killing our people!"

"Wow, but how did they find the village?"

"Morton discovered one of the labyrinths, and Simon, the dwarf wizard, opened it and helped them follow the path to our village."

"I'm very sorry to hear that. There must be something we can do… Thaddeus, it has to be," Andy replied.

"Well, master, there is one thing. Our orders are to gain as much time as possible, so the earliest we can open the Golden Gate is the day before the full moon cycle. Will you be ready?"

"Of course!" Andy replied, and then Thaddeus continued, "Vale and Kaleb will be waiting for us at the end of the tunnel. They went to see Fedora for instructions, and from there, we'll go together to the mountains to meet Nikos before we start our journey to find the Scepter of Julius."

"In that case, we don't have any time to lose…Oh, crap! I lost my dagger when I killed that monster!"

"Master, don't worry about that now; we must find the Scepter of Julius first."

******

Lucy had been enjoying her spring break on the beach with some friends, and the same night Andy had his disturbing dream, she had one, too. The next day, just by the time Lucious and Thaddeus appeared, she called her brother to see if everything was fine, and he told her, "Hey Lucy, the guys are back, and we have to open the gate on Saturday night instead of Sunday."

"In that case, I'll go back home on Saturday, and I've something to tell you and the dwarves, too."

"What is it, Lucy?" Andy asked.

"I'll tell you when I see you." She said, without imagining that she would have the same dream for the next three nights

Over the next three days, the dwarves updated Andy with all the sad news from Ethernia. He knew then that his confrontation with Zoltar was inevitable and began to feel the pressure, making it difficult for him to fall asleep. The dwarves had to use some magic dust so Andy could relax and sleep. The final task was ahead, and he needed all the rest he could get.

When he awoke on Saturday morning, he felt more relaxed, but something unexpected was about to happen. When he was having breakfast with his parents, his father told him, "Andy, after you finish breakfast, please get dressed and come and help me clean and organize the attic." Andy looked speechless and didn't know how to react. His first thought was, *what if my father discovers the music box?*

"Sorry, Dad, you said to go to the attic. Do you mean today?"

"Of course, today, son. Tomorrow, your mother and I are going to a BBQ at Mr. Jordan's (The Museum's President) house, and I'd like to tell him what we can donate to the museum. He told me that the Board of Directors plans to open a new room in your grandfather's name."

His father's request scared Andy more than a Panwolf running after him. *What should I do now?* He was thinking. If his father finds that music box and gives it to the museum, how will he open the gate to Ethernia? He had to think quickly.

Of course! Luscious and Thaddeus, they'll be able to help me! After being excused from the table, he ran to his room to get dressed and told the dwarves what his father wanted to do that morning.

"Guys, we have to do something! If he finds the music box, we're doomed!"

"Don't worry, master, we'll use an old dwarf trick on him, and he won't be able to see that black chest!"

After getting dressed, Andy met his dad in the attic, and over the next four hours, they sorted the items to be donated and cleaned the room. They passed in front of the black chest many times, but Conrad didn't even look at it. Then, he told Andy, "Son, I think that's enough for today. Your mother will review the rest sometime during the week to determine what we can donate or if she would like to keep anything. So, let's go and thank you, son."

Andy breathed a sigh of relief and went back to his room. He found his two small friends there and immediately thanked them for the trick they had played on his father, which had saved the day.

Later that afternoon, Lucy arrived home. After saying hello to her parents, she went directly to see her brother.

Andy was talking to the dwarves when Luscious suddenly said, "Lady Lucy is coming… just about now."

One second later, Lucy opened the door and said, "Hi Andy… guys, it's so nice to see you again. We have to talk, but let me freshen up a little, and I'll be back soon." Andy and the dwarves nodded, and she left the room.

A few minutes later, she returned, and Andy told her, "Well, Lucy, you said you have something to tell us."

She nodded and said, "I've been dreaming with you for four nights. Every night, the same dream. I don't know how to describe it. I saw different scenes, like visions. First, it was dark, and you were walking inside a tunnel with some dwarves. I heard some voices, but I couldn't recognize them. Then, there was a light at the end of the tunnel, and when you got closer, a shadow in the shape of a rose appeared. Then, you were walking in the snow, climbing a mountain. Someone was behind you, but I couldn't see their face. Some dwarves were following you, too. Next, you were inside a cavern full of ice, holding something like a lance or spear in your hand, and some dwarves were around you. When you were about to leave the cave, a dragon attacked you and the dwarves. You couldn't get out as the dragon was throwing flames at you, melting the ice around the cave entrance, blocking your way out, and trapping all of you inside. Then, suddenly, the mystery person appeared again and shot the dragon with a crossbow right through its heart, and the dragon died. The last part of the dream was the most disturbing. You were in front of a dark castle, fighting with a monster, when a dark knight threw a spear at you. Then everything became dark, and I woke up. Andy, I'm afraid some dangers are ahead for you. I don't know if you should go!"

"I don't have a choice, Lucy; I must help these people. What do you think, Thaddeus?" Andy asked, and Thaddeus responded,

"Lady Lucy, be sure that we'll be highly cautious and ready to protect the master with our lives if necessary. It seems that this dream reveals what may happen in the future; we must remain alert and recall what you just told us when the time comes. I'll try to find some more answers later."

"Andy, I'm going to rest for a while. See you at dinner. And you guys, I'll see you tonight! Bye," Lucy said as she hurried from Andy's room.

Andy and the dwarves couldn't hide their concern for that dream, especially Andy, who thought, *Maybe Lucy is correct, but these people need me... I'm the only one who can help them.*

Chapter Twenty-three: The Golden Crossbow

The dwarves assured Andy that they would be ready to protect him with their lives if necessary, and they would consult about Lucy's dream with Nikos when they arrived in Ethernia. Andy and the dwarves looked at each other without saying a word when Danny opened the door and said, "Hi guys…Ready for the next adventure?"

After closing the door, Andy pulled him in quickly and said, "Careful… my parents could hear you." That was the kind of distraction Andy needed to change his mood, and Danny seemed to master it.

Later at dinner, just as Mrs. Muller was serving the dessert, something awkward happened. They all heard someone knocking at the front door, and Mrs. Muller went to see who was there. When she opened the door, a cold breeze came inside the house, hitting Mrs. Muller right on her face, making her hair look as if she had seen a ghost. After she closed the door, a soft female voice was heard whispering, *"Andy… don't forget the golden dust."*

The three youths almost choked on their dessert and looked at each other with wide-open eyes. Andy nodded quickly at them, like a warning not to say anything, noticing his parents acted like they hadn't heard anything. But, when Mrs. Muller returned from the front door with her new hairdo, they couldn't avoid laughing at her -- even Conrad chuckled, covering his mouth with one hand. Helen reacted by giving everybody "the look." They stopped immediately. Then, she stood up to fix Mrs. Muller's hair, and Conrad changed the topic, asking Lucy and the boys, "Do you guys have any plans for tonight?"

"I'm going to stay home, Dad; I haven't had much rest this week!" Lucy told him.

"And you boys, the usual stuff?"

"Yes, Dad, nothing special. Watch some movies and play some video games," Andy said.

"Well, it seems like we all are going to have a peaceful night at home!"

Then, the three youths left the table and went upstairs to Andy's room. Danny and Lucy wondered what the new message could mean.

"What was that?" Lucy asked Andy.

"I know exactly what the voice meant; they wanted me to take the gift I got for my birthday," Andy said.

Thaddeus and Luscious were waiting for them in Andy's room. They knew the youths would come and ask for that strange voice, and before they even said anything, Thaddeus told them, "That was a message from the mermaids. They're the only ones who can produce that kind of sound. Do you have that bottle of golden dust?"

"I remember that voice," Andy said, and added, "It was the same one that gave me the warning in the forest, and yes, I have that bottle in my closet."

"Well, don't forget to bring it with you tonight. Are your parents going out, Andy?" Thaddeus asked.

"I don't think so. They didn't say anything."

Then Thaddeus said, looking at Luscious, "We have to put them to sleep early; every hour counts. We won't take any chances. So, we'll give them a little extra dust so they and the nice lady won't wake up until late tomorrow morning."

Lucy went to her room, and when she opened the door, she almost yelled as she found a beautiful green rose floating over her bed! Immediately, she turned back, ran to Andy's, and whispered, "Andy, Andy! Come quickly!"

Andy left his room and saw his sister there, very agitated. Lucy grabbed his hand and took him quickly to her room.

"You have to see this, Andy!"

"What's going on?"

When she opened the door, however, the rose was gone.

"But it was right here," she said.

"What was here?" Andy asked.

"A green rose floating in the air over my bed!"

They went to Andy's room, and when Thaddeus saw Lucy's face, he asked her, "Lady Lucy, what troubles you?"

"There was a green rose floating over my bed. I swear I saw it, and now it's gone."

"This is the second time you saw a rose; first, in your dreams, and now here in your chambers. I think this has to be a message. We'll see what happens tonight when we open the golden door."

Lucy wondered why that green rose appeared in her room. Like the others, she was anxious to go to the attic to see what the golden door would bring this time. A few minutes later, Andy's parents came up to say goodnight. It was unusually early for them to go to bed, but Luscious' special treat was starting to work, and they would be sleeping like logs in no time.

It was around 9:00 p.m. when the three youths and the dwarves went to the attic. Andy was already correctly dressed and wearing the Clover ring. Luscious was in charge of bringing the key, but this time, without noticing, he was closely followed by Chester, who, from the moment the strange voice was heard at dinner time, had been acting particularly weird.

"Luscious, what are you doing? Why did you bring him?" Andy asked.

"What, Master? Bring who? I don't understand!"

"Look behind you, Luscious," Andy told him, pointing at the dog.

"That's strange. Why did he follow me this time?" Then Thaddeus said, "I think I have the answer: He was the gatekeeper of the rose, remember? And you, Lady Lucy, saw the rose symbol twice. Maybe he wants to be with us in the secret place (the Attic)."

"I don't understand, but if you say so, let's go!" Andy said in a confused tone.

Seconds later, everyone, including Chester, was in the now half-empty attic. They took the music box from the black chest and placed it on the table. Then Andy opened it, and precisely as before, the moonlight came into the window, illuminating the music box. The green cloud began to appear on top, revealing the magic words Andy had called out twice.

AURA GATE… AURA GATE!

The room started to rumble. Once again, they didn't know where the door would appear. They looked everywhere until suddenly, the left wall of the attic began to open, letting the oval door come inside the room. Once again, Andy used the key to unlock it, and the emerald in the middle of the door opened again like a mouth, saying, in a firm tone,

WELCOME, MASTER; LET THE CLOVER TOUCH THE GREEN BEFORE YOU OPEN THE DOOR.

"What is this supposed to mean?" Andy asked, a little confused.

"Master, the stone wants you to touch it with the ring of clovers!" Thaddeus said

Andy closed his fists and touched the emerald with the ring; an ample green light came from it, and then the emerald spoke.

OPEN THE DOOR NOW, MASTER.

Andy opened the door, and as usual, the portal was there. He turned towards Lucy to say goodbye, and Chester started to bark, acting strangely. Then, the old dog stood between Andy and the gate, preventing him from entering the portal.

"Calm down, Chester! Let him pass!" Lucy said.

As Lucy tried to pull Chester out of Andy's way, a golden cloud appeared in front of the gate, and the dog moved out, clearing the way. A second later, the cloud vanished, and a golden crossbow appeared, floating right there. No one moved, looking flabbergasted at the apparition. Thaddeus quickly said, "Take the crossbow, Master!"

However, when Andy tried to grab the crossbow, he was rejected, feeling something similar to an electric shock in his hands. Turning to the dwarves, he said, "I don't understand. Why can't I grab it, Thaddeus?"

"That's very strange, Master. Why would the ring send this if you can't grab it?"

"Because it's not for you, Master!" Luscious said, pointing at the dog, grabbing Lucy's hand, and pulling her to where the crossbow was floating.

Then, Luscious added, "My lady, go and try to get the crossbow."

Lucy hesitated momentarily and slowly approached the crossbow, stopping right in front of it. Then, she paused for a long second, forcing Andy to yell, "Lucy, take it!" After a deep sigh, she finally had the courage and grabbed the crossbow, to everyone's surprise, without difficulty. Andy and the rest were stunned, and Lucy, looking at the crossbow, said, "Hey guys, it has a rose in the middle. Come and look!" And Thaddeus said

"This means you have to come with us, Lady Lucy. The rose has chosen you, and only you can use this crossbow. Now I know the meaning of your dreams and why your dog wanted to come to the secret place!" And then Andy interrupted, saying,

"No way; it's too dangerous. I'm not going to let my sister go!"

"Andy, you forget I'm your older sister, and I'm big enough to make my own decisions, so shut up! Now I understand my dreams… I was that mystery person whose face I couldn't see. I must go with you, and so I will!"

Danny, who had been very quiet, said, "Can I go too, guys? I want to help!"

"Master Danny, we need somebody here to guard the door and be with the prince and princess when they wake up. You're an important part of this task, too." Thaddeus told Danny, making him feel like a million bucks.

So, after saying goodbye, the siblings and the two dwarves crossed the portal, and the door started to close, leaving Danny alone in the attic with the music box.

******

Inside the portal, Thaddeus informed the group that they were heading to a different area in the forest, closer to the mountains, so it would take them a little longer to arrive. Lucy was walking behind Andy at the end of the group, feeling a déjà vu since she had seen the same scene in her dreams.

When they finally reached the end of the tunnel, it was already daylight in Ethernia. They had to jump from the edge, and Lucy was new to that. She saw the ground at least twenty feet below the tunnel.

Lucy got scared and hesitated, so Andy grabbed her hand and told her, "It's an illusion. It looks high, but it's no more than three feet high, so jump with me... Don't be afraid, and trust me."

Lucy closed her eyes and jumped with Andy. When they landed, she opened her eyes and chuckled. She told her brother, "You were right; the height was an illusion."

"I told you," Andy said.

Then Thaddeus interrupted them and pointed at some bushes, saying, "Kaleb and Vale should be here soon; let's go and wait for them behind those bushes."

After a few minutes, they heard a tiny voice saying, "Greetings, everyone." It was Vale and Kaleb, coming from Crystal Lake. Kaleb was carrying a beautiful rose, and when they saw Lucy, they both said at once, "You must be the one marked by the rose?"

Andy and Lucy looked at each other in surprise, and before anyone could say anything, Kaleb gave the rose to Lucy. After thanking the dwarf, Lucy was as stunned as everyone else when the rose turned red to green and vanished in her right hand. Everyone was speechless, but what happened next blew their capacity for astonishment.

Andy was the first to see something on Lucy's right arm and said, "Lucy, your arm is glowing!" She immediately uncovered her birthmark, and the perfect rose was genuinely glowing. Suddenly, she closed her eyes, and her entire body began to glow. She remained like that for a few seconds. When the glow disappeared, she opened her eyes and saw everyone staring at her with their mouths open.

"What happened, guys?" she asked, then added, "It looks like you just saw a ghost."

"Hey, sis… you don't remember anything?" Andy asked.

"Did I miss something?" Lucy said.

And Thaddeus answered, "The rose has found its chosen one."

"The good queen told us to give the rose to the young lady coming with you, carrying a golden crossbow, and the rose will do the rest…" Vale added, and then Lucy asked,

"By the way, what happened to my rose?"

Thaddeus answered, "It's inside you, my lady; you have been chosen."

The confused Lucy nodded in return, and after a short silence, Andy said, "We'd better get to Nikos at once!"

"Master, the secret passage is near, but we must be cautious; patrols are all over the forest, and now we're with Lady Lucy."

"You're right!" Andy responded, and the group began searching for the secret passage. Vale and Kaleb went ahead to see if the route was safe.

They reached the passage's entrance, and Thaddeus opened it with the new password, *"Lubirikus in."*

The wall opened, and Andy told Lucy, "Don't touch the bushes; they're poisonous, and don't make any noise that disturbs them, making them attack you." Lucy looked at her brother with wide, open eyes and nodded in understanding.

They crossed the passage quickly, arriving at the southwest end of the forest, about a mile away from the base of the mountains. Soon after, they arrived at an area surrounded by rocks and trees, and found themselves on what appeared to be the bottom of a cliff, which seemed like a dead end. But it was an illusion created to confuse possible invaders. It was the entrance to the cave where the dwarves had been refugees since Zoltar's army attacked their village.

Thaddeus said the unique password, and the group entered the cave. The dwarves inside looked at them, wondering who the human girl was. Lumi came up, and after greeting them, she asked, "Sir Andy, it's so good to see you again. Who is this lady who comes with you?"

"Hello, Lumi. This is my sister, Lucy. Please take us to your father. We need to talk to him."

"It's nice to meet you, Lady Lucy," Lumi said, and Lucy returned the greetings with a cordial smile.

Nikos was notified of their arrival and came out to welcome them. Since he didn't expect to see Lucy, he said, "Welcome back, Sir Andy. Who is this young lady?"

"Lord Nikos, allow me to present my sister, Lucy Logan. She's the one marked by the rose," Andy said while Nikos looked at her, still confused. Lucy showed him the perfect rose on her arm, and Thaddeus explained what had happened thus far. Vale and Kaleb added what Fedora told them about the mark made by the rose.

"My young Lady, welcome to Ethernia. We're so pleased to welcome you. Consider this village as your own home. " Many dangers lie ahead, and I hope you're prepared," Nikos responded, and after a pause, added, "Now, we don't have a moment to lose." I will join you in the quest for the Scepter of Julius. We'll leave after breakfast... Oh, Lady Lucy, my daughter Lumi will give you something to put on so you can conceal your strange clothes, and also will protect you from the low temperatures in the Icy Mountain."

Hot chocolate and muffins were served, and Lucy couldn't resist the delicious goodies. Nikos gave the final instructions to the messengers leaving for the two cities, preparing the loyalists for the upcoming fight. The brave Vale was sent again to see Fedora to confirm that Nikos, the two chosen ones, and the dwarf army would be by the lake as soon as they found the Scepter of Julius.

After breakfast, Andy, Lucy (Wearing a black cloak and a proper pair of shoes that Lumi gave her, not to look conspicuous), Nikos, and five more dwarves left the cave via a secret tunnel that took them directly to the desert part of the mountain. From there, it would take them more than a full day without stopping to reach the Icy Mountain. They didn't know that Zoltar had ordered Simon to send the dragons and some hawks to patrol the mountains, looking for the dwarves' hideout.

During the first part of the journey, they passed through a very deserted area of the mountains, composed chiefly of sand and rocks, with no sign of life. By mid-afternoon, they made their first stop to take some snacks, during which Thaddeus told Nikos about Lucy's dreams, and the dwarf lord's first question to her was, "Do you know how to use that crossbow, my lady?"

"No, sir."

"Well, in that case, you need to start practicing immediately. Come with me!"

"Okay, Lord Nikos," she said and followed the dwarf to an area where he prepared several targets for her to practice.

Lucy pulled the crossbow out of her shoulder, and Nikos taught her how to load and shoot the arrows. When she was about to shoot the first arrow, her birthmark glowed, and sudden energy filled her body, changing the expression on her face and making her eyes look like they were on fire. She began to hit every target Nikos chose for her with such skill that everyone looked at her, utterly surprised. After she hit the last target, Nikos finally said,

"You are marked by the rose indeed. Only you could use this crossbow with such skill and precision!"

Stunned by what she just did, Lucy responded, "Lord Nikos, I swear I've never used anything like this before!"

They continued their journey until they arrived at the snowy part of the mountains, where Lucy felt another déjà vu, looking at the same scene she had seen in her dreams. They still had a long way to go to reach the Icy part of the Mountains, so they didn't stop again to rest until later that night. It was cold, but they couldn't make a bonfire without risking being spotted. There, Nikos gave everyone a ration of the special biscuits he had prepared to help them with the cold, and after a short rest, they continued their journey.

They climbed the first mountain the whole night without stopping, and finally, almost at sunrise, Kaleb, who was ahead of the group, reached the summit, discovering what seemed like an entrance to a cave on the next mountain. He quickly called the others. Nikos was the last to get there, and when he looked at that cave, he said, "Good work, Kaleb; that has to be the one we are looking for; let's go. It can't be that far." Energized by the discovery and without a moment to lose, they headed to the next mountain.

It seemed close at first sight, but it took them over an hour to get there. When they arrived, Nikos asked everyone to look for a clover mark to confirm it was the proper cave. Andy found it at the bottom right of the entrance and said, "I found it. It's small, but it is a clear clover." And Nikos added, "Good work, master. Okay, everyone inside…quickly."

Andy and Lucy were the first to enter the cave, and as the rest were following them, a hawk appeared flying around that mountain, sent by the closest Goblin camp to patrol. The hawk saw the group of dwarves entering the cave, so it wouldn't be long before the bird would report what it had just seen to the Goblins in the camp.

The temperature was dropping inside the cave, and Nikos warned everyone, "We need to move quickly; we won't be able to stay here too much longer; the temperatures will drop more, and we may freeze to death!"

They lit two torches and began walking. After about five minutes, they found three new tunnels. Then, Nikos, who knew Julius, realized that he wouldn't make it easy for anyone to find that Scepter and said, "The one leading to the Scepter must be marked by a little clover hidden somewhere. We will surely face some traps if we take the wrong tunnel."

After they found the tiny mark in the tunnel to the right, they continued their march, finding even more tunnels, like a labyrinth. Each time they found a new group of tunnels, they had to look for the clover mark to choose the right one to enter and follow the path. Finally, they arrived at a large cave, where everything appeared to be frozen, and the temperature was extremely low. There was a huge piece of ice right in the middle, like a big rock; inside, it appeared to be glowing a deep red. Thaddeus saw it first and yelled to the others, "Right there in that piece of ice! There's something inside."

They quickly approached that piece of ice, and as they drew closer, the red dot inside and something under it that resembled a stick became more apparent. When they reached that big rock of ice, they saw the magnificent Scepter of Julius with a massive ruby in the center. The whole group stared at the only thing that could destroy the evil Zoltar. No one said anything for a few seconds, then Andy asked,

"How are we going to break this piece of ice?"

Nikos answered, "Don't travel yourself, Master Andy; Ionel and Octavius (the two dwarves added to this journey) have brought their pickaxes." So, he told them to start picking. However, they couldn't even scratch the ice. It was so big and heavy that they couldn't even move it; it didn't budge. They tried everything, but nothing worked.

Time passed, and the temperature dropped even more, so frustration was rising in all of them. Then Andy told Nikos, "There must be a way to break this thing. We didn't come this far for nothing. What should we do, Nikos?"

"Master, you're right; there must be some other way, but what...?" Nikos said.

Suddenly, Andy's ring began to emit a light. Lucy noticed it and yelled at her brother, "Hey Andy, look at your ring!"

"It's another message, Master. Take your ring off and see what it says," Nikos said.

Andy took the ring off and found another inscription: *"Only the power of the clover can release it."* Andy finished reading, and Nikos yelled, "Use the ring, Master; you must use the ring."

Andy put the ring back on his finger and made a fist. Then, he touched the ice with the ring, and a red light emanated from it, melting the ice quickly. Anxiety grew as the ice continued melting, and the Scepter looked closer and closer…

*****

At the goblins' camp, Simon and his two dragons arrived seconds after the hawk landed and reported what he saw. The camp Commander informed Simon about the presence of dwarves in the mountain. Simon immediately sent one of his dragons to attack and kill the dwarves.

******

The piece of ice continued melting, and the Scepter was only a few inches away. When Andy finally reached it, he grabbed it with his left hand, pulled it out, and instantly turned to give it to Nikos, who took the Scepter in his hands, and after looking at it, he said, "The Scepter of Julius. The only thing that can destroy the evil Zoltar. We have been waiting for many years, and finally, it's in our hands. Thank you, Sir Andy!"

Nikos returned the Scepter to Andy, who accidentally pushed the ruby, and a spear came out from the bottom of the Scepter. Everyone was amazed at the view, and Andy yelled, "This is it; the Scepter becomes a spear! This is the weapon to kill Zoltar!"

Everyone gathered around Andy and started cheering.

Then Lucy, feeling another déjà vu, remembered her dream and said, "Oh God, the dragon is next. The dragon is coming! Let's get out of here now!"

Andy saw Lucy's face and yelled, "She's right; let's go before the dragon blocks our way out." Nikos ordered the group to leave the cave, but wondered how a dragon could be there unless Simon knew they were there. They were going as fast as they could, with Kaleb in front. Suddenly, he made a quick turn, entering the wrong tunnel, and if not for Andy, who grabbed him, he would have fallen into a deep hole.

Finally, they saw the entrance and began running towards it. When they were about to exit, a huge flame burst, forcing them to retreat inside the cave. The dragon was just outside and sent another flame, making a big piece of ice fall and blocking a large part of the exit. Lucy grabbed her crossbow and yelled, "I need to get closer!"

"Do you remember where to shoot?" Andy asked.

"Yes. But I need to get a little closer," she said.

Lucy crawled to the exit, and as the dragon was about to send another flame, she shot the beast directly in the heart. The dragon roared in pain, raised his wings, and started falling in circles. Lucy, Andy, and the dwarves crawled out of the cave and left using the small open space at the entrance. Right after the last dwarf exited the cave, another piece of ice fell, covering the entrance completely.

When they were all out, everyone cheered Lucy. Andy hugged her while the dwarves gathered around the siblings in one big group hug…

Chapter Twenty-four: The Battle for Ethernia

Nikos interrupted the celebration, saying, "That dragon was sent by Simon, thinking only some dwarves were here; his spy didn't see me or you and Lady Lucy; otherwise, he would have come himself, or even Zoltar. Now, the dragon won't return, so he'll come to look for it and will find that golden arrow on it. We must move quickly and reach the secret passage as soon as possible."

Quickly, the group began to descend the icy mountain, heading back to the forest. After traveling the whole night without resting, they reached the lower part of the mountain just before dawn. Suddenly, out of nowhere, three giant hawks attacked them. They ran to the closest rocks to protect themselves, but they weren't big enough to hide all of them. Nikos directed his attention to a group of trees about a hundred yards away and yelled, "We need to get to those trees! We may be able to open the secret passage from there."

When they ran in that direction, one of the dwarves, Ionel, stumbled on a rock and fell. At that moment, one of the hawks grabbed him from his legs and started pulling him up.

"Help... help!" Ionel desperately yelled. Lucy saw it and immediately pulled the crossbow, and when she was ready to shoot, Nikos yelled at her,

"You have to shoot the hawk in the head; otherwise, he'll drop Ionel, and the fall may kill him!"

Andy and some of the dwarves went on to distract the other two hawks, so Lucy quickly aimed and shot the one carrying Ionel right in the head. The hawk closed his claws, raised his wings, and started falling. Nikos, Luscious, and Lucy ran to help Ionel before the hawk hit the ground. The other two hawks retreated, giving them enough time to get to the trees, where Nikos yelled the password, *"Lubirikus in."*

They entered the passage one by one, and just after Andy crossed carrying the wounded Ionel, the other two hawks returned, ramming at the entrance shortly before Octavius could get in. The Dwarf used his blowpipe to hit the first hawk, but couldn't avoid being attacked by the second. Andy left Ionel with the others and came back to help Octavius. Using the Scepter of Julius as a spear, he pierced the hawk's heart, killing it instantly, but Octavius, who was already wounded, told him, "Master, leave me here. I'll slow down your journey!"

"No way, Octavius. We started this journey with you and will finish it with you!" Andy affirmed

They crossed that passage as fast as they could; Andy was carrying Octavius, and the others were helping Ionel. They had to reach the village quickly before Simon discovered the dead dragon, so every second counted. After almost an hour, they finally reached the end, and Nikos yelled, *"Lubirikus out."*

The passage opened a few yards away from the dwarves. The guards at the entrance came to their aid and escorted Ionel and Octavius inside to receive treatment. At the same time, Henrietta and the rest of the dwarves enthusiastically received Nikos and the human lads.

******

Early that morning at the goblin camp, an extremely concerned Simon jumped on the other dragon and flew to the Icy Mountain. He was looking for the one he had sent the day before, but it hadn't returned. When he got to the summit, his dragon roared and pointed down. Then, Simon saw his other beloved dragon lying on the ground and ordered his dragon to land beside the dead one.

When they landed, he stood by the dead dragon and, biting his teeth, said, "**Whoever did this to you… will pay. I swear!**" Then, he saw the golden arrow in the death dragon's heart and thought,

A golden arrow; I haven't seen anything like this before. I have to show this to Zoltar; he may know who's behind this! He took the arrow and ordered the dragon to fly back to Ambrosia.

When he arrived, he went immediately to see his master, who asked him, "Simon, any news? Did your dragons find anything?"

"Master, I found one of my dragons dead, with this in his heart!"

Simon showed Zoltar the golden arrow, and the color of Zoltar's face changed completely. His eyes were ready to blaze.

"What is this? A golden arrow. Someone found the golden crossbow." Simon, afraid of Zoltar's reaction, was trembling as he asked, "What do you mean, Master? I don't understand."

"You idiot! You never understand! The golden crossbow has been hidden for centuries! It was a gift from Julius to the Rose family, from which Nolan is a descendant. Whoever possesses this weapon never misses, but it has to be someone chosen by the crossbow. Perhaps

Henrietta used the ring of clovers to locate the crossbow and give it to the chosen one that everybody talks about. I must find them before they do anything against me! Tomorrow morning, we'll start executing those damn dwarves at dawn and sunset, ten at a time, until they tell us where the rest are hidden."

******

After taking a much-needed rest, Andy and Lucy were summoned by Nikos to start preparing for their journey to Crystal Lake. All the remaining warriors were there, too, including Lady Henrietta, who also wanted to be part of the fight. They didn't have silver dust anymore, so Nikos prepared a lotion to help them block the trolls and Panwolves' sense of smell so they wouldn't be detected if they hid in the forest.

Lunch was served for everyone, during which Nikos gave final instructions before leaving for the lake; for safety reasons, they split into two groups. The first, led by Nikos, had the humans, Luscious, Thaddeus, and approximately twenty warriors go to the lake, while the second, led by Kaleb and the rest of the Army, would proceed to a point in the forest and await further instructions. Nikos' group would have to go through two secret passages for this journey, which would take them longer. However, the route was safer, except for the final part, since the second passage ended about two miles from the lake, an area heavily patrolled by Morton's army.

It was getting dark when Nikos' group finished crossing the second labyrinth. As soon as everyone was out in the forest, Nikos ordered them to put on the special lotion and be alert. They started heading for the lake; moments later, a large patrol was sighted.

Quickly, they hid in the bushes, and Nikos whispered to Andy and Lucy, "Don't move!" Everyone held their breath as the patrol passed. Nikos's lotion was doing its job, blocking the trolls' and Panwolves' senses; the goblins wouldn't be a problem. The patrol passed without noticing them. Lucy looked on in shock as she gazed at these giant, ugly creatures. Andy had to shake her twice to make her react. She looked at him and said, "Andy, pinch me… I must be dreaming."

Andy chuckled, and Lucy whispered, "I can't believe what I'm seeing. First dragons, now goblins and trolls, and finally, those Panwolves. It's like being inside a fantasy book."

"You haven't seen anything yet, sis; wait till we get to the lake," Andy retorted

The group continued marching through the heavy foliage and was closer to the lake; fortunately, they didn't encounter another patrol. By then, Andy couldn't hide his emotions. He was about to see Marily again, and his heart started beating faster with every step.

When they arrived at the protected area, Nikos said the unique password, and the group got in, barely missing a second patrol that passed only a few yards away. The protected area was covered up to fifty yards wide from the lake shores, and no patrol could get in or see what was inside. Upon arrival, they rested while waiting for the Queen, who would take some time to appear.

After almost an endless hour, when everyone fell asleep, a huge splash came from the lake, followed by the shell chariot emerging from the waters with the queen and the princess. For the first time, an escort of at least eight mermen surrounded the chariot. All of them were armed with their tridents, ready to protect their queen.

Lucy stared in astonishment at the magnificent view, but nothing could prepare her for what was coming next. Just before they left the chariot, the Queen and the Princess touched their fins, which turned into human legs. Lucy almost fainted, forcing Andy to grab her before she fell to the ground. Then, Fedora spoke.

"Good to see you again, young sir. I see you have the Scepter of Julius; well done, and I suppose the young lady with the golden crossbow is the one marked by the Rose." Then, turning to Nikos, she added, "My friend, it's good to see you and your people here, as well. This lady must be Henrietta of Utopia; it's good to see you're well, too."

After all of them bowed to the queen, Andy introduced his sister. "Your Majesty, Princess Marily, allow me to present my sister, Lucy Logan."

Lucy bowed to the queen and said, "It's an honor to meet you, your Majesty!"

Fedora nodded and returned the salutation with a smile and said,

"Welcome to Ethernia, Lady Lucy; it's good to have you here." Then Lucy changed her attention to Marily. She confirmed how beautiful she was and noticed how the mermaid princess and her brother had been looking at each other.

Marily addressed the two siblings. "Hello Andy, it's so good to see you again, and Lady Lucy, it's a pleasure to make your acquaintance."

"Hello, Marily, I'm happy to see you again," Andy answered.

Lucy added, "Nice to meet you too, Princess Marily. My brother has told me so much about you. Please call me Lucy."

At the end of the formalities, Fedora went directly to business, explaining the task and revealing her plans for it: "We don't have a moment to lose. The Oracle has spoken and told me we must be at Ambrosia before dawn. Zoltar will start executing dwarves until somebody tells the location of the remaining dwarf nation, or… all the dwarves give themselves up! Your approach has to be through the river so I can protect you with my power. I have two boats ready for you. These boats will be invisible to anyone outside them; Morton has an army of goblins and trolls camped between the forest and the city, close to the river. We must attack them first to prevent them from defending the city. I will send my army with you, two hundred of my best mermen. They will transform into warriors as soon as they get out of the river. Each of them possesses the strength of five men, but since it requires a significant amount of power for their transformation, it will last no more than half a day. Then, they must get back to the water. You will send the rest of your army to meet them at Morton's camp. Nikos, your group, and twenty of my warriors will continue to the city. I will also send the seagulls to help you; the rest will be up to you. You must get Sir Andy closer to Zoltar."

"Excellent plan, Fedora. You've covered everything. I'll send a message to Kaleb to move the rest of our army close to Morton's camp by dawn and wait for our signal to attack. We must leave now and let justice prevail!" Nikos said.

"One more thing, Nikos; my daughter will go with you. She wants to fight, representing our people!" Following those words and with a simple wave of her Scepter, Fedora made a magic bow appear with a set of blue arrows and gave both to Marily, who took them. She approached Andy and, taking his hand, told him, "I'll be by your side at all times." Andy smiled and pressed Marily's hand tenderly.

The two boats prepared by the queen emerged from the waters. The first was bigger, so Andy, Lucy, Marily, Luscious, Nikos, Henrietta, and about twelve dwarf warriors got on. Thaddeus, Vale, and the other six warriors were in the second boat. They left as Fedora returned to the waters. She wanted to observe everything through the Oracle and see how she could help from there.

The boats were crossing the lake, covered by the darkness of the night, followed by Fedora's army. When they reached the Crystal River, Fedora's spell started to work, and the two boats became invisible. From that point, they were about two hours away from their first stop, Morton's camp, and everyone was already anxious and eager to fight.

When Andy showed the Scepter of Julius to Marily, she saw an inscription in tiny letters. They were so small that it was difficult for the human eye to see them, but not for a mermaid. Then she told him, "Look, Andy… there's something written here!"

"What do you mean, Marily? I only see an engraving."

Marily read, "Only the one who bears the ring must use the spear against the dark."

Nikos, who was listening, told him immediately, "Master, it means only you can use this Scepter to kill Zoltar because you're the bearer of the ring. You must face him and cross his heart with the spear. Remember that as long as you have the ring, he can't kill you, but he may try to enchant you, so you have to be careful."

Andy remained silent for a moment and then said, "Well... I must do what I must...I'm ready!" His expression changed, showing him more determined and focused than ever. He started showing why he had been chosen as the Keymaster, and everyone looked at him confidently and respectfully.

Finally, the boats reached the point where they had to separate; they were about half a mile from Morton's camp. The first boat with Andy's group and about a dozen mermen had to continue the journey down the river, heading directly to the entrance of Ambrosia City. When they arrived, they were surprised to find a few guards there. The dwarves took care of them quickly using their poison darts, while a group of loyalists was waiting close by to give some clothes to the mermen so they could disguise themselves as peasants. Andy, a bit confused, asked.

"Why such a little garrison?"

"Everybody is at the square for the executions. It will be carried out as soon as the sun rises," one of the people said.

"We have to hurry up!" Nikos exclaimed.

At that time, and not so far from the city, a vast cloud was crossing the sky, heading in that direction. It wasn't a regular cloud; it was the seagulls, thousands of them, sent by Fedora to help in the attack on the city as the Queen had promised them.

Nikos ordered the group to go fast to the main square, where the first ten dwarves were about to be executed. When they got there, taking advantage of the large crowd, everyone quickly took their positions around the square. Andy and some of Fedora's warriors were among the people in the center. Nikos and Henrietta were hidden in one corner, with Luscious and some dwarves. Finally, Lucy, Marily, and a group of the best archers from the lake were taken to the top of the houses surrounding the square, where they aimed their arrows at the executioners.

Simon, who was presiding over the execution, read Zoltar's proclamation,

"By orders of our supreme Lord Zoltar, all dwarves have been declared traitors and will be executed unless they swear absolute loyalty to him and provide information about the location of their leaders and the rest of their people." A drum roll followed Simon's words, and just when the roll ended, the sky turned dark, and an immense "**Awe**" from the crowd was heard. It was the cloud of seagulls blocking the sun.

Simon looked up, and when he saw the seagulls coming down, he immediately lowered his thumb in a signal to proceed with the execution. A yell of horror came from the crowd, and just as the executioners standing on the platform were about to kick the benches off for the dwarves to be hanged, arrows were shot directly at their heads, killing them instantly.

Andy and the mermen ran to liberate the prisoners while the seagulls attacked the trolls and goblins in the square, creating total pandemonium. The people reacted by yelling some hurrahs; some even joined the fight against the monsters. Then, Simon started sending spells to kill the seagulls and everyone approaching him, but when he saw Nikos coming in his direction, he ran to the castle, looking for his master.

The evil lord was still in bed and snoring when a servant abruptly awakened him. The servant yelled, "Master… master, we're under attack! The people are taking the square!"

Zoltar jumped out of bed and screamed, "What? Where's Simon?! Call for the guards!"

Zoltar was ready to start the battle when Simon got to the castle. "Master… Nikos and the humans are attacking the square, and the people join them. Thousands of seagulls are there also, attacking our troops," Simon said

"Nikos, eh… and with that boy, the chosen one, get Morton's army quickly! I'll personally take care of this rebellion! I have been waiting for this moment for a long time!"

******

By then, at Morton's camp, his army had been completely caught by surprise; the dwarf and mermen armies were fighting magnificently, commanded by Thaddeus, Kaleb, and Vale. In a few words, they were kicking Morton's army's butt. In a masterful execution of Fedora's plan, the dwarves attacked the Panwolves first, putting them out of combat; then, each merman was fighting with up to three goblins at the same time; they were faster, and their tridents more potent than the goblins' weapons; while the dwarves were getting the clumsier and slower trolls. When Morton saw his camp practically defeated, he escaped with an escort of goblins, running to the city.

Morton was running like a chicken chased by a wolf, thinking the attack was only on his camp. Then he saw Simon coming his way, accompanied by a small escort. They looked at each other in surprise. Morton told Simon about the attack on his camp, and Simon responded, "What! The army has been reduced, and the city is under attack, too! Let's go back; the master probably has everything under control. We'll regroup there!"

******

In the city, Zoltar was dealing with the seagulls, using his arms as flamethrowers, burning as many as he could, while Andy's group and the people of Ambrosia were marching to the castle after they had overtaken the trolls and goblins at the square. They were about to meet Zoltar's guard and test the power of the evil lord.

Pushed by the crowd, Andy, Marily, and Nikos were advancing to the castle; the other dwarves and mermen were following them, too, but it was difficult to pass through Zoltar's guard. Lucy and Marily were shooting at the guards, but they were so big and strong that the only way to kill them was to shoot them right between the eyes.

Then one of the guards shot an arrow at Lucy, and Luscious, who was right by her side, threw his body to protect her, taking the arrow right in his chest. Lucy quickly shot the guard right between the eyes, killing him instantly, and turned to attend to Luscious; she tried to get the arrow out of his body, but it was too painful, and the dwarf told her, "My lady, don't worry about me. Protect yourself; follow the others quickly before the guards attack you. Go now… go!"

"I can't leave you here! You'll die for sure!" she said, but he insisted, and Lucy went after the others. Two other dwarves came to help Luscious.

When Simon and Morton returned to the city, they ordered their escort to defend the gate and not let anyone in. Thaddeus and part of Fedora's army were right behind them and arrived just in time to defeat the guards and enter the city.

By then, Zoltar was already out on the streets, and his guards were opening the way for him, killing whoever was trying to get closer. In the middle of that chaos, Andy got a glance at Zoltar, but when he was about to get closer to him, he was attacked from behind. It was Morton who arrived at the scene and threw his lance, barely missing Andy, but grazing his left arm, cutting it, and making him fall to the ground. Morton pulled off his sword and got closer to finishing off Andy when Nikos ran to defend the boy and received a mortal wound from Morton's sword. Marily, who was right behind Nikos, shot Morton right in the head with two arrows, killing the monster in seconds. Andy regained composure and grabbed Nikos, who was mortally wounded, and said to the boy, "Sir Andy, you have to finish this! Please…don't let the evil lord get away. May your gods help you?"

Andy could hardly contain the tears and answered. "You have my word, Nikos, I will,"

Then he heard a voice saying, "Go get him, Sir Andy; I'll take care of Nikos!" It was Henrietta arriving at the scene.

Zoltar, who saw with pleasure what had just happened to Nikos, began to walk toward Andy. He was waving his arms, throwing out of the way whoever was trying to interfere. Marily saw him and, without delay, shot one of her blue arrows at him, but Zoltar quickly disintegrated the arrow in the air with a finger move. In retaliation, he sent a flame to Marily that made her fall badly; he didn't know she was Fedora's daughter. Otherwise, she would kill her. Andy got so pissed that he immediately regained his focus and went on to confront Zoltar. Suddenly, and practically out of nowhere, Simon appeared from behind Andy, ready to stab him with a lance, but then Thaddeus quickly pushed him out of the way. The dwarf wizard turned to face Thaddeus and, sending a powerful spell, threw him quivering to the floor. Simon quickly picked up his lance, and when he was about to kill Thaddeus, a golden arrow shot by Lucy pierced his heart. The dwarf wizard collapsed and looked at Thaddeus, whispering, "My master will avenge me."

Andy finally got closer to Zoltar. They were separated only by a few yards. Zoltar was the first to hit, throwing two balls of fire at Andy, who managed to avoid them by moving very quickly. Then Zoltar snarled, "You think you can run from my power? You haven't seen anything yet!"

The Evil lord ordered the dragon to attack the invaders, and he sent another spell that threw Andy back, falling on his wounded arm and causing him to lose the Scepter. Thaddeus quickly came to help him get up and gave him back the Scepter. Andy regained his strength and firmly walked toward Zoltar, this time, aiming the Scepter at the evil lord, who at that moment sent another spell to Andy, but the protection of the ring combined with the Scepter made the spell reflect on Zoltar, and it hit him badly. Then Zoltar, realizing he couldn't harm the young lad, began harming the others around him. He sent mortal spells to everyone closer to Andy. Then he saw Lucy and Marily;

Andy noticed that and yelled to them, "Lucy, Marily. Get out of here... **NOW!**"

Moving fast, the two girls avoided a mortal spell sent by Zoltar, but Lucy was barely touched on one of her legs, receiving some burns. Andy tried to distract Zoltar before he could do more harm. He made the spear come out of the Scepter and pointed it at Zoltar, without knowing that in doing so, he sent a fireball at him. Zoltar blocked that fireball and immediately wondered. *He has the Scepter of Julius; I must have it.*

Zoltar knew then that he needed to do something else to take the Scepter from Andy. Thus, he thought, *it looks like he cares about those girls; I shall take at least one of them; he'll give me the Scepter for her life!* Zoltar got his opportunity very quickly when Marily got closer to help Lucy. Andy saw the evil lord's intentions and tried to get there before him, but it was too late; Zoltar's dragon grabbed Marily and came to pick up the evil lord. Andy couldn't get any closer because the dragon began throwing flames at whoever got closer, burning them on the spot. Then, Zoltar jumped on the dragon and yelled, "The girl for the Scepter, or she will die! HA, HA, HA!" And then he flew to the highest tower in the castle.

Ahhhh!! Andy yelled in frustration, but something struck his mind. He felt the little bottle with golden dust in his pocket, and he remembered the note: "Use the golden dust to beat your final task." Andy pulled the bottle out, closed the spear again, and gently threw the dust on himself, starting to float in the air. Then he yelled, "I can fly." So, he went after Zoltar, who was already in the tower with Marily. When Andy got to the closer window, he could hear the princess saying, "You're a coward. You couldn't face Andy by yourself!"

Andy stood in one of the windows and yelled at Marily to get away from Zoltar, who immediately threw a spell at him, making the lad almost fall out of the window, but Andy quickly grabbed one of the curtains and regained his position.

"If you want the girl alive, give me the Scepter!" Zoltar said.

"No, Andy, don't do it! He'll destroy everything!" Marily yelled.

"I don't have a choice, Marily. All right, Zoltar, you win, but on one condition. You'll give me the girl first, and I'll give you the Scepter!" Andy responded

"You aren't in a position to set any conditions, boy. If you don't give me the Scepter now, I'll kill her right in front of you!"

"Andy, don't do it, or he'll destroy you too," Marily yelled.

Andy was a clever boy. Suddenly, he figured out how to get closer to the evil lord and said, "Zoltar, I'll give you the ring, too, if you give me your word that you won't harm the girl. But you know that I have to give it to you voluntarily."

"You have a deal, boy. Come and give me the ring and the Scepter!"

Andy began walking toward Zoltar very slowly. The evil lord looked at the boy, thinking, *I'll be invincible with that ring and the Scepter...and yes, I won't harm the girl, but you will pay for this, boy.*

Marily was crying and begging him not to do it. Andy pulled out the ring and kept it in his left hand, and with the Scepter in his right hand, he started to get closer to Zoltar, ready to make the exchange. When Andy was about to give Zoltar the ring, he noticed how the evil lord was staring at it with a greedy expression. Thus, Andy took advantage of Zoltar's distraction and pointed the Scepter at the evil lord and pushed the ruby in the middle, making the spear come out and skewer Zoltar's heart.

"Goodbye, Zoltar. I hope you burn in hell!" Andy said, biting his teeth.

Mortally wounded, Zoltar grabbed Andy's shoulder, and with fire in his eyes, he pronounced his last spell. "PIETRUS INSTANTE"

With those words. Andy began to turn into stone, as Zoltar was still grabbing his shoulder and melting like the Wicked Witch of the West. Marily screamed in horror at the sight of Andy turning into a statue. `

Andy could remove Zoltar's hand from his shoulder, but couldn't stop the spell. In a few seconds, he turned into stone, and Zoltar completely vanished, leaving only his clothes on the floor. Marily, still in shock, hugged the frozen Andy and started crying. She embraced that cold statue for long seconds without knowing what to do. Her heart was broken.

It seemed at that moment that no force in Ethernia would separate her from Andy's stone body. After a few seemingly endless seconds, something incredible happened. The statue began to feel a little warmer, so the confused Marily let go and stepped back. Utterly astonished, she saw the statue slowly turning back to normal, and her eyes began to glow. She was looking in disbelief with her mouth open when all of a sudden, Andy winked at her, and opening her eyes in surprise, she responded with a big smile. They embraced in a long hug and kissed each other several times until Marily told him,

"Oh, Andy, you're back! I thought I'd never see you again!" She kept touching his face, and with tears in her eyes, she asked him, "How did you break the spell?"

Andy lifted his eyebrows and slowly opened his left hand, showing her the ring of clovers. Marily smiled in relief, and Andy said,

"I'm glad I kept it in my hand; the ring's power was stronger than Zoltar's spell, and it saved my life. Ohhh…how good it is to feel your hands again," Andy said and kissed her.

By then, at the front of the castle, everyone was still fighting, unaware of the turn of events in the tower. However, suddenly, something happened that gave everyone a sign that the evil lord had been defeated. Everything created by Zoltar started to disappear. The guards, the goblins, and the trolls were converted into dust in front of the stunned crow. Then, Andy and Marily approached the window and started yelling,

"Stop fighting… The dark lord is dead…Zoltar is dead!" making everyone outside explode into cheers.

Then, something unexpected happened. The dragon approached Andy and bowed to him as if in gratitude for killing Zoltar. The beast then allowed Andy and Marily to mount on his back and brought them down to the ground. The final transformation began when they landed, and the horrible, dark castle transformed back into the beautiful one it had been before.

Everyone there watched in astonishment as everything unfolded. Zoltar's reign was finally over, and the people could smile again. The sky opened up utterly, revealing the sun's entire splendor, making it the most beautiful day in this land in a long time. In front of the castle was a magnificent view; Andy and Marily had the dragon by their side. Andy raised his spear as a sign of victory.

Then everyone around the castle began celebrating, cheering their savior's name, "Sir Andy…Sir Andy…Sir Andy." Humans, dwarves, and even the mermen from Fedora's army all gathered around, yelling as one

Chapter Twenty-five: The New Beginning

Back in the attic, Danny was falling asleep, even though Nolan and Morgana were talking to him to keep him awake. Suddenly, a huge tremor was felt in the room, making Danny abruptly awake and almost falling off his chair. Nolan and Morgana didn't know what to do. Then, the music box began to float in the air. The prince and the princess grabbed each other, and the emerald in the middle of the door spoke firmly.

"OPEN THE DOOR, YOUNG MASTER ...THEY HAVE TO GO NOW!"

Danny was so afraid he couldn't move a finger. Then Nolan yelled at him, "Do what he said. Something must have happened. Open the door!"

"But where will you go? I'm supposed to protect you!" he said.

"OPEN THE DOOR...IT'S TIME," the emerald spoke again.

Then, snapping out of fear, Danny jumped up and opened the golden door. The music box closed and went through the portal, disappearing from Danny's view. Everything happened so fast; he looked as shocked as the guy whose numbers won the lottery that day, but he had forgotten to buy the ticket. Then, the emerald told Danny,

"THANK YOU, YOUNG MASTER...WELL DONE!"

For a few seconds, he remained frozen, not knowing what to do. Finally, he reacted, wondering where they had gone. *What am I going to tell Andy and Lucy?* He didn't have a clue that all of this was happening because of Zoltar's death. The prince and princess would finally be free.

The music box spun around inside the tunnel, crossing it at breakneck speed. Nolan and Morgana hugged each other, not knowing what to do; many things were on their minds... Then Morgana started to talk, almost in panic, "My love, I'm afraid something terrible has happened, and this could be the end!"

"Don't even think about that; I know all this is very strange; let's hope the young knight fulfilled the prophecy. Otherwise, I don't think the door will open so easily."

The box was spinning faster and faster; Nolan and Morgana were wondering what would happen to them next.

******

At the front of the castle in Ambrosia, everybody gathered around the triumphant Andy, who, with all the commotion, had forgotten the pain in his injured arm. Lucy, limping, came to congratulate his brother and Marily, and the three embraced in a long hug. Lady Henrietta, who was standing by the lifeless body of Nikos, also got closer and, full of emotion, hugged Andy as well, but squeezed his injured arm a little bit, making him bleed even more. Suddenly, the pain hit him, forcing Andy to grab his arm, and Henrietta exclaimed,

"Sir Andy, you are hurt; we need to tend your wound."

At that precise moment, a lovely humming melody was heard, grabbing everybody's attention, followed by a cold breeze that made everyone look at each other, like asking what was going on. Suddenly, a small blue cloud appeared in front of the group surrounding Andy, and an image formed under that. A familiar voice was heard seconds later, and the image got clearer. It was Fedora, the Queen of the Lake, who, using the power of the Oracle, appeared to see the final triumph of the people of Ethernia over the evil Zoltar.

"Bravo, young Master, you've just fulfilled the prophecy. This land is finally free from Zoltar, and we are eternally grateful to you. Today is a day for a celebration; our prince and princess will join us in a few moments!" Fedora said

"Thank you, Your Majesty, but I couldn't have done it without the help of all the people around me now. All of them deserve to share the credit as well!"

"Always showing class and humility; you are a brave knight, Sir Andy!"

At that moment, a group of dwarves brought the bodies of Luscious and Nikos for everyone to pay their respects, and then the queen said, "These are our true heroes, and they will always be remembered. Now it is up to us to show that their sacrifice hasn't been in vain and rebuild this land they helped to set free!"

Then the queen noticed that Andy and Lucy were wounded and added, "You lads must be cured immediately." Fedora swung her Scepter again, and a basket of water leaves appeared there. The queen said, "Cover your injuries with these leaves. In a few hours, you will be well."

When Fedora finished saying those words, a strong wind blew, and Fedora yelled, "They are coming!" Then, a small twister appeared right in front of the queen. As the twister vanished, the beautiful music box slowly descended from the air until it landed on the ground.

There was a deep silence for the next few moments; no one dared to speak. Finally, the music box opened, and the two little princes floated out of it and began to grow…and grow back to their regular size. The crowd looked amazed and in joy at the last two heirs to the thrones of Ambrosia and Utopia, appearing after centuries of being enchanted on that box.

When the prince and princess were fully grown, they looked confused to see everyone staring at them. Henrietta couldn't contain her emotions and ran to hug them. After so many years, she was finally seeing them again. Then the Queen of the Lake said out loud,

"People of Ethernia, here are your rightful rulers, Princess Morgana of Ambrosia and Prince Nolan of Utopia! With them, fairness, goodness, and justice will return to this land."

An explosion of cheers erupted from the crowd. Everyone there knew the prophecy had been finally fulfilled. Both princes bowed to Fedora, who returned the protocol with a smile. After looking around, Prince Nolan sighed and spoke to the people.

"Dear Subjects, the evil lord has been defeated, and we are all free at last. Goodness and justice have prevailed. Let's spread the news all over the realm." Then, pointing at Andy and Lucy, he continued, "We must thank these two people. They came from their world to help us, and we should always remember them."

Cheers and hurrahs were heard after Nolan's words. Fedora applauded in approval and then addressed the two siblings,

"Sir Andy and Lady Lucy, you'll return to your world when your injuries are completely cured. That will take a few hours, so we'll meet by the lake tomorrow morning to give you a proper goodbye. Now, my people must return to the water, and you need to rest."

Then, the image of Fedora vanished, and the mermen began disappearing. Marily came close to Andy and, after kissing him very tenderly on the mouth, told him, "Till tomorrow, Andy. You have been brave, and I'm very proud of you!" Waving at Lucy, Marily disappeared as well.

The siblings approached Nolan and Morgana to congratulate them for being free at last. Then, once again, the ring emitted a light, which got Andy's attention. He removed it from his finger to read the new inscription, and looking at Nolan and Morgana, he said, "Our mission here has ended, and I believe I won't need this anymore. It belongs to you now." Andy gave the ring of clovers and the Scepter of Julius to Nolan, who, after taking them, read inside the ring:

"To the rightful King of Ethernia"

"Thank you, Sir Andy. I will wear it proudly. I invite you and your sister to spend the day with us at the castle, celebrating this victory. We'll escort you to the Lake before you return to your world tomorrow morning."

Then, Lucy asked them, "Well, guys, when is the wedding?"

Both princes answered, "Very soon."

******

Something amazing happened at the cave where the rest of the dwarves were taking refuge, too. The black cat that Zoltar enchanted started to transform back into Alina, Princess Morgana's loyal servant. When the dwarf people saw that transformation, they knew the evil lord had finally been defeated and began cheering as well.

When their leaders returned from the battle, they immediately began preparations to relocate their village to the forest, closer to the Lake. Unfortunately, they hadn't heard the news about Nikos yet.

Thaddeus and the dwarf warriors left the city just before the beginning of the celebrations. They took the bodies of Nikos and Luscious back to their people for a proper funeral, but before leaving, they promised to be by the lake the next day to say goodbye to Andy and Lucy.

******

Early that night, the people of Ambrosia began to celebrate all around the city; the bells of the castle rang after many years, without stopping, announcing the victory over Zoltar. Messengers were dispatched to Utopia and all the villages in between to give the great news. The prince and princess took possession of the castle, and their first announcement was their upcoming wedding and the unification of their two kingdoms. Following that, they announced a national holiday to celebrate the freedom of the land.

Andy and Lucy went to their rooms, where they rested until their wounds healed. A few hours later, after donning more appropriate clothing, the siblings joined the celebrations. A feast in their honor was prepared in the castle; laughter and music returned to this land for the first time in centuries. It was like the happy ending of a fairy tale;

people were dancing in the streets, and at midnight, a show of fireworks (The ones used to entertain Zoltar every night) was displayed, this time to the joy of everyone, closing the first day of celebrations.

When Andy and Lucy woke up the following morning, everything seemed like a dream, but it wasn't, for they were still in that fantastic castle. The whole experience of the last few days hit them all at once. Then, they realized the magnitude of what they had just accomplished and how they had done it, so they felt overwhelmed, especially Andy. Killing the evil Zoltar was still unfathomable for him. Thus, when they saw each other before coming down for breakfast, they embraced for a long time, and Andy said to her sister, "We did it, Lucy… I'm proud of you, and I love you!"

Lucy shed a few tears and said, "I love you, too, little brother."

After enjoying a delicious breakfast with Nolan, Morgana, and Henrietta, during which they had the chance to learn more about this beautiful land, they all left the castle, heading for Crystal Lake, accompanied by a small delegation from the city. On their way to the lake, they witnessed a remarkable transformation. They saw how the Shire and the Emerald Forest regained their original splendor overnight. They were stunned to discover the beauty of this magical land, a beauty that only Henrietta, Morgana, Nolan, and the dwarves had known.

When they arrived at the lake, Alina and the dwarves were already waiting for them, and the loyal servant was the first to run towards Morgana, "My lady, how wonderful it is to see you again!"

"Oh, my loyal friend, this is a happy day; I never thought I'd see you again," Morgana cried.

Then, Alina bowed to Nolan, who smiled and hugged her in gratitude for her loyalty. Next, Alina was face-to-face with Lady Henrietta. Both looked at each other and couldn't contain their emotions, crying and embracing in a long hug.

Following that tender moment, Andy, Lucy, Morgana, and Nolan approached the dwarf delegation to present their condolences for the loss of Nikos and Luscious. The dwarf delegation was presided over by Liona, Lumi, and Thaddeus, who was about to be named their new leader. For the next few minutes, everyone presented their respects to the dwarf delegation, and more than one tear was shed; even Andy had to rub his eyes and wipe away a couple of tears, his sadness doubled. He lost a close friend in Luscious and a guide and mentor in Nikos.

Suddenly, a big splash on the lake got everyone's attention. The shell chariot was emerging from the water, bringing Fedora and Marily, followed by an escort of mermaids and mermen.

After turning their fins into legs, Fedora was the first to touch the ground, followed by her daughter, Marily. Of course, all the attention turned to the Queen and Princess from the Lake, who immediately approached the group and, facing Andy and Lucy, said,

"Sir Andy and Lady Lucy, Ethernia will be eternally grateful to you, and as a token of our appreciation and gratitude, I have these presents for you."

Marily gave her a golden shell, and the queen pulled out two beautiful pendants, which she placed around Lucy's and Andy's necks**. She added, "These pendants are a gift from the people of Ethernia; they'll protect you if you ever need them**." Andy and Lucy thanked and bowed to the queen.

Then Marily approached Andy and, after kissing him, said, "I hope you'll never forget me because I won't forget you. You'll always be part of my heart."

Andy, pressed by the emotion, hugged her and said, "I won't forget you, Marily. This is for you!" He took his medallion off (a gift from his grandparents) and placed it around Marily's neck. Stunned by the gesture, Lucy thought, *Let's see what Mum will say about this.*

Finally, it was Nolan and Morgana's turn. They approached the siblings, and Nolan said, "Please keep this and always remember us. This is the symbol of what you have done for us." He signaled his escort to give Andy the music box, the same one where he and Morgana had been prisoners for centuries.

The two siblings were visibly emotional. After thanking Nolan and Morgana for the gift, Andy said, "We'll never forget you…you'll always be in our hearts… Goodbye, friends!"

Just before Andy could say the magic words to call for the little twister, Lucy gave the golden crossbow to Nolan and said, "You are its rightful owner, King Nolan." And to everyone's surprise, a beautiful red rose appears floating in front of her.

The crowd gave a loud cheer as she took it, and then Fedora said, "The power of the rose has paid the young lady for such a noble act."

Everyone stepped back, making room for Andy, who raised the golden key one last time and said the magic words, **AURUS WIND... AURUS WIND, COME TO PICK THE GOLDEN KEY!** The Aurus wind appeared, and the two siblings waved their hands, saying goodbye to everyone, and jumped into the little twister that took them to the tunnel back home.

******

In the attic, Danny was in panic mode. The music box was gone! He didn't know what had happened with his friends and wondered what he would do if nobody showed up before sunrise.

At that moment, Andy and Lucy were inside the tunnel, getting closer to the golden door. They were talking about their beautiful experiences in Ethernia and the gifts they had received. Andy told his sister, "Lucy, this must be our secret; only Danny should know."

She responded, "It's a shame we can't share this wonderful experience." Then she yelled, "Oh my God. Why didn't I bring my camera?! We could've taken a lot of pictures!"

"You don't know if your camera would work there. Remember, it's a magical world, and chances are you won't be able to record anything. The important thing is that we helped them, and they're free now." Then Lucy, in a sadder tone, added, "The question is, what are we going to do tomorrow? No more dwarves, no more clues, no more fun."

Then, Andy replied, "Something else will happen, sis... don't worry now."

When they arrived at the door, Lucy told Andy, "Bro…we have been gone for six days. What are we going to tell Mom and Dad now?" Andy replied, "Nothing. Remember that only about six hours have passed here, so it must be around 3 a.m."

Andy opened the door slowly, and on the other side, Danny, not knowing what he would face, was shaking like an earthquake and covering his eyes. Then, the two siblings crossed the portal. When they put the music box on the floor, before they could say anything, Chester, the loyal dog who spent the night in the attic, ran to greet his masters, wagging his tail and jumping all over them. Andy and Lucy hugged and petted him, and both told him, "Good boy, Chester, good boy. Yes… We miss you, too!

Danny heard that and felt a sudden relief. He uncovered his eyes and ran to hug the siblings. "Holy crap. You two are alive! I'm so happy to see you! You can't imagine the things that happened here…but wait, what are you doing with the music box?" he yelled.

Andy said, "Yes, we know, dude. The music box was gone, but I brought it back."

The golden door began to close very slowly behind them, and in a soft tone, the emerald said.

"PLEASE, MASTER, RELEASE THE GOLDEN KEY." Andy pulled the little key out of his pocket, and the emerald opened like a mouth for Andy to put the key inside; then the emerald said,

"THANK YOU, MASTER, GOODBYE NOW…AND GOOD LIFE TO YOU TWO…"

The door disappeared through the same wall from which it had come. The three youths stared at their connection with the magical world of Ethernia for the last time. An empty feeling invaded them, and then Danny asked, "So, did you fulfill the prophecy? Tell me, I'm so anxious to hear the whole story."

"Yes, dude. I killed that bastard; all the spells disappeared, and the land is free now, but I wouldn't have done it without Lucy. That's why the music box was taken from here, by the power of the ring, and the prince and princess…I mean, the king and queen now are free, and they gave us the box as a gift!"

"Wow, so you two did it! Bravo dude! You too, Lucy. But, please, tell me how everything happened?"

"Let's put everything in its place, and I'll tell you everything in my room. Lucy needs to rest, too," Andy told Danny, and then put the music box back in the black chest. When he was doing that, Lucy noticed that the music box didn't have its lock and said, "Andy, look, the lock is gone; it disappeared when you returned the key."

"Wow…you are right, no more links to Ethernia."

When they finished with the attic, the boys went to Andy's rooms, and Andy began to tell Danny the story of their last journey to Ethernia. Danny listened in fascination; it was like a movie. It was almost 5 am when Andy finished, and they were so tired that they fell asleep in seconds.

By then, Lucy was already asleep, holding her beautiful pendant with her right hand. Then, a few minutes later, two familiar figures showed up: Vale and Kaleb, the new messengers sent by Thaddeus, the new dwarf lord.

Their mission was to put some magic dust on our friends. This would make them believe the whole thing had been only a dream. Vale went to Lucy's room, and Kaleb to the boys'. When they were ready, they dropped the dust on them, saying,

"Rest, my dear Master/Lady… In the morning, you'll believe you just had a nice dream. The pendant will be gone, but it will return to you soon."

After that, the two dwarves disappeared, and the three youths continued sleeping, having a pleasant dream.

******

They only slept a few hours, but the magic helped them to wake up well-rested. It was around 10 a.m., and Andy told Danny while yawning, "Ohhhhh… dude, I slept so well, I had a very nice dream."

"Ohh, I had a nice dream, too, and now I'm so hungry."

"Oh, crap! It's Sunday, biscuit day! We'd better hurry before Helga gets mad!" Andy yelled.

When they were at the table, Lucy joined them, looking well-rested. The three youths talked and laughed like nothing had happened the previous night. After breakfast, Lucy went out with her mother to go shopping, while Andy and Danny went to the movies that afternoon, as everything seemed to be back to normal.

The following day, as the boys were boarding their school bus, Andy saw a new girl sitting in the back. For a second, he held his breath as she looked mighty familiar. He sat with Danny, and on their way to school, he couldn't take his eyes off her, turning to see her several times. Danny noticed and asked him, "Hey dude, what is it? You've been looking at that girl since we got on the bus!"

"I don't know. She looks very familiar. I know that face, but I don't know where I've seen her before!"

"She's pretty," Danny said, and then added. "It's the first time I've seen her on this bus. She's probably a new student, so I don't think you've seen her before!"

"I'm telling you, man, she looks mighty familiar!" Andy retorted.

Later that morning, when the boys entered their history class, they saw the same girl. This time, she looked at Andy and gave him a little smile. When they were all seated, the teacher told the students, "Boys and girls, we have a new student. She just moved here from Scotland. Her name is Emilia Gavriland, and she is referred to as Emily. Please come forward, Emily, and say hello to the class."

She came to the front of the class to say hello, and once again, she looked at Andy with her beautiful green eyes. Suddenly, Andy remembered his dream and had a strong déjà vu feeling; then, like a lightning strike, he unconsciously yelled, "Marily…!"

Then, the teacher corrected him. "Emily, her name is Emily." The rest of the class laughed, and Andy, when his face turned red, didn't know where to hide it. That girl was identical to Marily (the mermaid of his dream). Andy couldn't believe his own eyes.

When class ended, Andy approached her and presented himself, "Hi, my name is Andy Logan. Excuse me, but have we met before?"

"Hello, Andy. It's a pleasure to meet you, too. You're funny, but I don't think we've met before. I just came from Scotland a couple of weeks ago!" she said in a very Scottish accent, and then Andy said.

"I saw you on my bus this morning. Where do you live?"

When she mentioned her street and number, Andy's first reaction was to say, "Wow…we are neighbors; you are only a few blocks from my house."

Since it was lunchtime, Andy walked her to the cafeteria and spent the lunch hour with her. During this time, they connected well and even exchanged phone numbers.

At the end of the school day, they sat together on the bus and spent the whole way home talking and getting to know each other. Danny was seated behind them, wondering what type of bug bit his friend this time. Why was he so interested in this new girl? When the bus got to Andy's stop, Andy said goodbye to Emily, telling her, "I'll call you later."

When he and Danny were walking to their homes, Andy said,

"You won't believe this, but I saw that girl in my dreams last Saturday! She was a mermaid called Marily. She looks exactly like her! I don't know, dude… but I think not only do I know this girl, but I have feelings for her, too!"

"That's impossible, dude!" Danny responded.

"We'll talk later. I'm confused now. Bye!" Each one went to their respective homes.

Andy, of course, was wondering about Emily. The more he thought about his dream, the more vivid the feeling became, and he got even more confused. When he got home, as he was saying hello to his mother, she noticed something and asked him, "Andy, I don't see your medallion. Where is it?

"I don't know, Mom, I realized at school that I wasn't wearing it; I'll look for it."

That was a gift from your grandparents."

"I know, Mom… I'll look for it…"

"Okay, son… Come with me now; I want to show you something. I went to the attic this morning and looked at what I found!" They went to the living room, where Andy saw a beautiful Music Box atop one of the tables. He looked at it, amazed by its beauty, and felt another déjà vu.

His mother said, "Look how beautiful it is! It must be old and valuable, too. I don't know why I didn't see it before. It must have been in the attic for years."

"You're right, Mom. It's indeed beautiful." Feeling a little strange, Andy excused himself and went to his room. That old music box was another thing he remembered from his dream.

Later, at dinner, when the whole family gathered, Conrad made an announcement.

"I have some news! I've been invited to a history symposium at Aberdeen University in Scotland this summer. I think it'd be an excellent opportunity for a family vacation and to visit our old home, Logan Place! How do you like that?"

"I think it's great, dear. It'll be very nice to visit the place where your family comes from," Helen said. Then, for the rest of the dinner, the family spent the time planning the upcoming trip.

Later that night, when everyone retired, Helen came to Andy's room and gave him a gift, saying,

"Son, I also found this in the attic. I think it'll look nice on you. I have one for Lucy, too." And she gave him the pendant that Fedora had given him, which was hidden by the dwarves to be found by her inside the music box.

Utterly flabbergasted, Andy responded, "Thank you, Mom." Suddenly, the whole dream came back to his mind.

He looked at the pendant briefly, and something made him call Emily. When she answered, he began telling her about the dream he had had a couple of nights before. First, he told her she looked exactly like the mermaid he met there. She laughed and said,

"Wow, Andy… you have a great imagination… and weird too." Then they switched the conversation, talking about why she moved to America and where she came from in Scotland. When she said her family was from Aberdeen, he said,

"No kidding. My family comes from there, too. What a coincidence." The conversation lasted a few more minutes, and then they made plans to go to the movies on the weekend.

After hanging up the phone, Andy went to bed feeling even more confused. Too many coincidences and many questions were spinning around his mind.

Why do I think I've met this girl before? She looks precisely like Marily, the mermaid... Could it be possible that they're the same person? Did I dream all this, or did it indeed happen?

Then he smiled, closed his eyes, and fell asleep. ...

The End

www.ingramcontent.com/pod-product-compliance
Lightning Source LLC
Chambersburg PA
CBHW030254100526
44590CB00012B/398